# MICHAEL STROGOFF

Thomas Roberdeau

# Michael Strogoff

*A Screenplay*
*based on the Jules Verne novel*

∾

WITH AN INTRODUCTION
BY PAUL SCHMIDT

LOS ANGELES
SUN & MOON PRESS
1995

Sun & Moon Press
A Program of The Contemporary Arts Educational Project, Inc.
a nonprofit corporation
6026 Wilshire Boulevard, Los Angeles, California 90036

This edition first published in paperback in 1995 by Sun & Moon Press
10 9 8 7 6 5 4 3 2 1
FIRST EDITION
©1995 by Thomas Roberdeau
Introduction ©1995 Paul Schmidt
All rights reserved

This book was made possible, in part, through an operational grant from the
Andrew W. Mellon Foundation, and through contributions to
The Contemporary Arts Educational Project, Inc.,
a nonprofit corporation

The author wishes to express his gratitude to the following individuals
for their generous support of this book project: Allen Daviau, Lee Edmundson,
Frank Simeone, Nick Frangakis, Sander Johnson, Chris Condon, Greg Donovan,
Devreaux Baker, and especially, Solange Baker Roberdeau.

Cover: Kasimir Malevich, *Red Calvary* (1928)
Cover Design: Katie Messborn
Typography: Guy Bennett

LIBRARY OF CONGRESS CATALOGING IN PUBLICATION DATA
Roberdeau, Thomas
Michael Strogoff/A Screenplay
p. cm —
ISBN: 1-55713-098-1
I. Title. II. Series.
811'.54—dc20

Printed in the United States of America on acid-free paper.

## Introduction

There are times when the world seems to go to hell over-night. One minute form, boundaries, recognizable rhythms, reliable definitions, the certainty of a day of rest at the end of the week. Then suddenly it all goes shrieking together, images collide like a hundred billboards jammed together on a commercial strip, and we get so dizzy we have to pull over and put our heads between our knees to keep from puking.

That's where we are now. With culture in America, I mean. Dizzy. If you want to call it vertigo and think it might make an exciting esthetic principle, go ahead. It's a vision, that's for sure. Visual, anyway. We are image-obsessed. That's why screenplays are so interesting.

We ought finally to face it: the screenplay is the major literary form of the late twentieth century. Almost all books nowadays, fact or fiction (if the distinction even exists anymore) are written with an eye to the screen, structured so that they can be turned into movie scripts overnight. But can the film script by itself, unmade yet into a movie, tell us anything? Can it push language into the visions it envisages, or does that push make language ultimately pointless? At what level in the process of transformation from screenplay to film does vision occur?

The text that follows is a screenplay, something that makes sense mostly in terms of its pictures, but of course they aren't there yet. You have to conjure them up. And the problem is, the conjuration can produce pictures that look like pictures you know already. Can we ever read a screenplay and imagine something new?

Tom Roberdeau tries. He tries to force language to produce pictures so powerful we can never have imagined them before: to create pictures, or rather the emotion pictures cause in us, through the medium of words.

Some of Roberdeau's pictures are disturbing. These are apocalyptic visions. Disaster is the on-going condition, inescapable, deepening from page to page.

> JOLIVET: "Into our hearts go mad songs / The ringing of which we bear / Yet only our sweet angels keep smiling / For the rest of us are stained with tears!"
>
> STROGOFF: What are you doing here?
>
> JOLIVET: Sending my last message before the world falls completely apart.
>
> (scene 108)

In this war story he has invented and re-interpreted, we begin to understand Roberdeau as one of those late Romantic rebels against modernism, someone who thinks of violent disaster as the matrix out of which authentic being can be engendered. That's why the grand, romantic, adventure screenplay is his natural medium.

What interests me so much in this text is the return to forms we've known for a hundred and fifty years, the classic simplicity of nineteenth century melodrama. Here comes Jules Verne, trailing his cosmic disasters and megalomaniac villains, and these then become the stuff of Roberdeau's transforming imagination.

But the big question he faces, we all face, is this: is it possible to avoid irony, the distancing device that modernism installed to keep us from the horrors of the modern world? It is irony, after all, that keeps us from puking there by the side of the road. It was modernism's saving grace. And yet irony keeps us from authentic experience. Is it possible to avoid irony, to diminish the distance? Perhaps, Roberdeau suggests, another century may serve, and he throws us head first into the stew of the nineteenth. Grand melodrama, he maintains, can transport us from the soul-stunting effects of irony. Violence, pillage, rage, fire, disaster, nature-worship, heroics, magic— who would have thought the last century's popular legends would save us?

Ultimately, I suppose, it's all futile. Was there ever a time, in art or in reality, when violence was really cathartic? If so, is this why we are so drawn to warrior tales?

When the hero staggers to his feet dripping with blood, his own and his enemy's, with a sense of triumph? With a sense that he'd really changed anything? Is triumph even the word? Perhaps only in the mad victory of survival.

But where else could you find a hero who kills a deer and eats it as a prelude to love-making? For this is high romantic adventure, and love is the only thing that makes the violence worth while. Consider this scene:

> *There's a low full moon. Michael gallops across its face.*
>
> *He reaches a stream and stops to rest. The moon is reflected. For an instant, Nadia's face seems to appear…her long hair like seaweed, her expression that of drowned death.*
>
> *Tears fill Michael's eyes.*
>
> *Then he kicks the horse, and they gallop across the stream, the hooves shattering the ripples.*
>
> (scene 95)

"Drowned death." Even Poe never used a figure of speech like that. But the scene! The moon, the Ondine figure in the water, the obsession and the galloping!

All this offers us the chance to live on a heroic scale, to confront violence and danger and remain true to something—to Nadia, to the Czar. The fantasy begins to crumble if we begin to consider the plot as a political statement, or if we allow irony to intrude. The glorification of that historical nonentity, the Russian Czar—how do we first see him? "The Czar is enraged. In crown and robes, he's an impressive figure." But irony teaches us to remember the historical nonentity beneath the crown and robes. That his arch-enemy Zurevno is a fascist in the d'Annunzio mold doesn't make the autocracy of the Czar any more legitimate. Yet our hero, Michael, goes through hell inspired by loyalty to this figure of inept authority.

Michael battles the glorification of individual power in the villain, Zurevno.

> ZUREVNO: There are men who are special, they're
> born this way. I always knew I'd be a fine
> soldier. I even had a head for strategy as a
> young boy staging snowball fights with my
> friends. I always knew I'd make history and
> that all of Russia would admire my name.
> My task was to grasp control over the situa-
> tions I was involved in....
>
> (scene 90)

And yet, can we not apply the same description to Michael himself? There's the trap of Romantic iden-tification, it teeters always on the brink.

And yet we are grateful for an artist willing to risk the grand gesture, trying to get to the *beyond* of things.

> CARETAKER: This is a time when we'll see many
> strange things on the road. You mark my
> words.
> NADIA: Why do you say this?
> CARETAKER: The world is not what it seems, Miss.
> That's all I mean.
>
> (scene 56)

But that's enough. If modernism gave us anything, it was the sense that the world was what it seemed, no more, no less—although how ironic, of course, that it was the way it was.

Tom Roberdeau wants the world to be more than it seems; he looks for a moment of transcendent experience that will yield up the mysterious truth of things.

Paul Schmidt

*But it is not the history of his success, but the history of his trials, which deserves to be related.*

—JULES VERNE

1876

*…sometime too hot the eye of Heaven shines….*

—WILLIAM SHAKESPEARE

## 1. OMSK, SIBERIA - EXT/NIGHT

*A dark sky over the small town. The full moon glows on the new snow, buildings all in silhouette. Chimney smoke circles in the air.*

*Silence. Suddenly the clicking sound of a telegraph. Through the window of the Telegraph Office, a lamp is lit. The Operator comes awake. An Old Man, wrapped in blankets.*

## 2. TELEGRAPH OFFICE - INT/NIGHT

*He rubs his eyes, turns up the lamp. Sits quickly at the desk watching the telegraph message. He blows his cold fingers. The formal message comes clicking on the line. The Old Operator writes it down on paper as fast as he can.*

*Abruptly the message stops. The Old Operator can get no response from the machine.*

*He curses and stares out the window into the night. His eyes drift upward to where the wires enter the office.*

*Suddenly the thick wire slashes across the glass, startling him. It whips in the cold wind, loose and dangling wild.*

*The Operator curses again, throws off his blankets, puts on a thick fur coat. He stares again at the hanging wire, then takes a long drink from a keg of vodka. He grabs his tool-box and goes out into the cold.*

## 3. NEAR OFFICE - EXT/NIGHT

*The Old Operator trudges through the snow. He looks up, sees the wire dangling in the sky above the office. He traces it with his eyes to the near pole. The wire is completely severed.*

*The Old Operator walks several yards toward the next pole, source of the problem. He's cold, and snow fills in the air.*

*He looks up and is shocked. A Tartar Renegade sits high on the pole, wirecutters slicing the line. The wire whips down at the Operator. The Tartar quickly leaps to the snow and stands before the Old Man.*

*The Renegade glares at him, then smiles gloatingly. The Old Operator drops his tool-box and runs in fear. The snow weighs him down as he struggles to get away.*

*Suddenly before him are Four Tartar Horsemen. The Leader, Feofar Khan, scowls at the weak Russian.*

*The Old Operator falls in the snow, rises, runs another direction. Feofar Khan's Lieutenant, Murga-Ti, raises his pistol. But the Khan shakes his head, then draws his saber and spurs his stallion forward.*

*He runs down the Operator, his horse galloping across the Old Man's wake. The Russian is petrified. Feofar Khan swings his sword savagely.*

*Red blood anoints the white snow. The Operator's head rolls. The decapitated body crumbles in a heap.*

*Some Tartars begin to chop down the pole. Others ride silently toward the town.*

## 4. A SIDE STREET - EXT/NIGHT -
   AT THIS SAME TIME

*A Woman and Young Girl hurry through the cold. They head toward the Telegraph Office. The Young Girl lags behind, trying to wrap her shawl tighter.*

WOMAN: Anna, we must hurry.

GIRL: Momma, it's so cold!

WOMAN: I want to be there when the message arrives. Don't you care about your father?

GIRL: Is he coming home?

WOMAN: I don't know. That's what the message will tell us.

GIRL: If he loved us he wouldn't stay away for so long.

*The Woman stops and grabs the Girl, shakes her violently.*

WOMAN: Never say that, Anna! Your father serves the Czar in his army, and the army needs him. He will come to us when he can.

GIRL: I'm sorry, Momma. Will he be here for the Holy Day?

WOMAN: I pray to God that he will. Now stop this crying
or the tears will freeze your face.

*They hurry on. They reach the Telegraph Office and knock
on the door.*

## 5. TELEGRAPH OFFICE - INT/NIGHT

*It's dark inside. The Woman keeps knocking, the door then
the window.*

WOMAN: Mr. Pasha! Are you there?

GIRL: Momma, are you sure it is tonight?

WOMAN: Of course, Anna! I've been waiting for this word
for days! Mr. Pasha?

*The Woman tries to see through the window glass, rubbing
the snow away with her mittens. The Girl tries the door, and
it opens.*

GIRL: Mr. Pasha?

*They step through the door. The Renegade Tartars grab
them and throw the Woman to the floor. She's petrified. The
Girl is held, she struggles, then a Tartar smashes a rifle-butt*

*against her head. The Girl slumps unconscious.*

*Tartars are wrecking the telegraph. Feofar Khan burns papers. Murga-Ti watches as his Men rape the Woman, but his eyes look on the Young Girl with affection.*

*The Woman cannot scream. Hands cover her nose and mouth as the Tartars work her over. The last man strangles her just as he is taking his pleasure.*

*They carry out the unconscious Girl. Feofar Khan spills the lamp, dousing oil over all the papers. Flames spread. The Telegraph Office is engulfed in fire.*

## 6. THE OUTSKIRTS OF OMSK - EXT/NIGHT

*The Tartars ride away, leaving flames far behind them. Murga-Ti carries the Young Anna across his saddle.*

*Galloping across the steppes, they leave a trail of wrecked telegraph poles and mangled wires in the snow.*

∾

## 7. MOSCOW - EXT/NIGHT

*Domed cathedrals adorn the skyline. Tall obelisks, minarets, and large walls surrounding a great fortress, the Kremlin.*

## 8. THE KREMLIN, JAIL TOWER - INT/NIGHT

*Through rusted bars, Colonel Zurevno stares at the stars. He appears calm, but his hands are working. He almost has the long steel nail out that holds the window in place. It twists in the stone. His fingers bleed as he works, digging with a rusted sliver from a bar.*

*His eyes watch the iron door. The nail makes a scraping sound so he stops, careful not to be heard.*

*He goes to the iron door and listens. Silence. He wipes his bloody hands on his pants, then returns to the work.*

*Through the bars he sees the Palace. He hears distant chamber music, and this makes him smile grimly. It also makes him work at the nail with more strength.*

*Finally it gives. He pulls it from the wall. It's almost a foot long, rusty but sharp.*

*Suddenly, he hears footsteps. Someone is coming to the cell on the other side of the door. He sticks the nail into his shirt and leaps into his cot, covering himself with blankets as if asleep.*

*The eye-slot in the door slams open. A Guard's eyes peer in and see him faking sleep.*

GUARD: Colonel, wake up.

*Zurevno groans under the blanket.*

GUARD: Wake up, I say! The Bishop is here.

*Zurevno sits up, rubs his face, pretends to awaken.*

ZUREVNO: The Bishop? Then my request has been granted?

GUARD: Stand to the far wall.

*The Colonel goes near the window, his back hiding the small hole the nail made. Keys rattle, the huge door opens.*

*Two Guards look around cautiously, then let the Bishop enter.*

*Zurevno sinks to his knees, head bowed reverently. The Bishop extends his hand, the Colonel kisses it.*

GUARD: Father, we'll be just on the other side of the door. Call me when you've finished with him.

BISHOP: Yes. Thank you. I'll be fine.

*The Guards take one last look, then leave, locking the door again. The eye-slot opens quickly, eyes make another check, then it slams shut.*

ZUREVNO: Thank you for coming, Father.

BISHOP: You have sinned, Victor Zurevno. God is angry with you.

ZUREVNO: Yes, Father.

*The Colonel rises, stares at the Bishop, who tries to be kind.*

BISHOP: Why did you ask for me, Victor?

ZUREVNO: I want forgiveness, Father.

BISHOP: The Czar plans to sentence you to death. He has told me so. You have plotted against him. How can you possibly be forgiven?

*The Colonel seems remorseful. He paces the cell, but the Bishop stays calmly seated.*

ZUREVNO: Father, I asked you to come because I wish to atone for what I've done. You are wise. We have known each other for years, you knew my family....

BISHOP: You were a fine officer once, Victor. You served the Czar valiantly in many battles. What possessed you to turn against him? What demon took you over?

ZUREVNO: I don't know, Father. I was angry at his policies. I was confused....

BISHOP: Perhaps Victor Zurevno believed that he should rule? Perhaps he believed he should be Russia's Czar himself?

*The Colonel smiles and shakes his head, implying this is foolish. But there's a gleam in his eye. The Bishop is becoming uncomfortable in the damp cell. He nervously fingers his ornate robe.*

ZUREVNO: Have you any word of my friends?

BISHOP: Victor, all the officers you led in the revolt have been put to death.

*Colonel Zurevno struggles to contain his rage.*

ZUREVNO: They were shown no mercy then.

BISHOP: Victor, God could do nothing to help them.

ZUREVNO: What can God do to help me?

*The Bishop thinks this over.*

BISHOP: I don't know, Victor. But you must be the one
to ask Him yourself.

*The Two Men stare at each other, as if in a challenge.
Then the Bishop goes to his knees. Zurevno remains still.*

BISHOP: Have you forgotten how to pray, Victor?

*Zurevno shakes his head. The Bishop stares in sympathy,
then bows his head and clasps his head in prayer.*

BISHOP: Father, in Your name I ask that You consider
this sinner, Victor Zurevno. He has unjustly con-
spired against the State, but I believe that somewhere there is goodness in his heart.

*The Colonel's eyes never leave the Priest. He slowly, silently
starts to circle the cell.*

BISHOP: Father, Victor Zurevno comes from an old and
honorable family. He is one of our flock, yet he
has strayed far from the righteous path. He asks
tonight to be received in Your grace.

*The Colonel has crept completely behind the Priest, who doesn't notice.*

BISHOP: Dear Lord, I, too, ask that you open Your glory to receive Victor Zurevno. I, too, pray that in Your divine wisdom—

*Zurevno leaps onto the Bishop, his arms around his neck, his hands over his mouth. He digs his forearm into the Bishop's throat. With all his strength he twists the Bishop's neck, and it snaps.*

*He keeps hold of the body as it slumps to the floor. Zurevno quickly stares at the iron door, but all seems quiet. He frantically pulls off the Bishop's robe and cloak, and he puts them on. Then he lifts the body to the cot and covers it with blankets.*

*Zurevno readjusts the Bishop's ornate robe so it covers his own clothes. He slips the hood over his head, ties it tightly to shield his face.*

*He kneels as if to pray in the same spot as the Bishop had. The long nail is held hidden and ready. Then he knocks on the door.*

*The eye-slot opens. The Guard sees "Zurevno" on the cot and the "Bishop" praying, his back to the door. The Guards locate their keys—*

*Zurevno grips the nail. Beads of sweat cover his face—*

*The Guards enter and Zurevno turns and leaps. He sticks the huge nail into the eye of the First Guard. Blood spews out, the Guard screams and falls.*

*Zurevno is quickly at the Second Guard, who draws his pistol. But the Colonel smashes it against the stone wall. It falls from the Guard's smashed hand. The Two Men wrestle.*

*Zurevno is very strong. He reaches out and grasps the First Guard's fallen sword, and the blade runs the Second Guard through.*

*The First Guard is crawling down the hall, blood flowing from the nail which penetrates his skull. Zurevno slashes. When the body is still, he hauls it into the cell with the others.*

*He struggles to get control, wrapping the Bishop's robe tightly around him and the hood that blocks his face. He conceals the weapons, then carefully makes his way down the hall.*

## 9. JAIL COURTYARD - EXT/NIGHT

*Guards bow to the "Bishop"/Zurevno, who hurries by. He blesses them and they're satisfied.*

*A Solder holds the Bishop's horse. Zurevno mounts. Then he slowly rides off with the dignity of a Churchman.*

*The gate is opened without question. Zurevno blesses Other Guards with his gesture of the Cross. Then, far enough away, he spurs the horse and gallops to freedom.*

es

## 10. THE PALACE, GRAND BALLROOM - INT/NIGHT

*Beautiful chamber music fills the hall. Aristocrats waltz with eloquent movements. Women are dressed in extravagant gowns. Men wear glittering uniforms or stylish suits. There's drinking, feasting, and laughter under glimmering chandeliers.*

*Jolivet, the French Journalist, cuts a piece from the huge cake shaped as Russia's Two-Headed Eagle. He drinks wine and watches the Women.*

*One Woman obsesses him, a bosomy red-head. The more he drinks, the more he stares. She dances with a Cossack Officer. Jolivet approaches them.*

JOLIVET: Madame, it will be my pleasure to dance with you, and it will be yours, as well. Sir, pass on.

*The Cossack is perturbed. The Woman smirks but is thrilled. Jolivet takes her hand.*

JOLIVET: Madame, you reflect great beauty tonight.

*He tries to kiss her hand, she lets him, then his lips climb, kissing her arm. He's so drunk he slips to the floor. The Cossack signals Two Servants to remove Jolivet. They hustle him off the floor, and sit him down on a sofa.*
*The Cossack and Red-head continue to dance. Jolivet applauds for them. A Servant passes by, and Jolivet grabs another glass of wine from his silver tray. He drinks and toasts the Servant, then Dancers.*

JOLIVET: I love you people! I love you to death!

*Jolivet takes out his sketch pad and pencil and begins to draw. Although drunk, his artistry is unaffected. The Dancers come alive on paper.*

## 11. THE BALCONY ABOVE - INT/NIGHT

*Czar Alexander watches his guests below. But his face shows worry, not merriment. General Nerensky whispers urgently into his ear, trying to be heard above the music.*

NERENSKY: It has been confirmed, Sire. The Bishop is dead. Also two guards.

CZAR ALEXANDER: How could this have happened?

NERENSKY: I don't know.

CZAR ALEXANDER: I curse the day Victor Zurevno was born!

*The Czar is enraged. In crown and robes, he's an impressive figure.*

NERENSKY: There is other grim news, Sire.

CZAR ALEXANDER: Tell me.

NERENSKY: We believe the telegraph lines into the Siberian frontier have been cut. We've been sending dispatches for several days, but many towns do not answer.

CZAR ALEXANDER: Could it be the weather?

NERENSKY: I wish this were so, Sire. But in truth, I believe our worst fears have come to life.

*The Czar is silent, thoughtful. He watches his guests, but he's oblivious to their pleasures. His eyes are tired, concerned.*

*Suddenly Czarina Catherine enters with her Attendants. She comes along the balcony toward the Men. The Czar admires his Wife's great beauty and eloquent gown. Jewels glitter in her hair and from an extravagant necklace at her throat.*

CZAR ALEXANDER: My wife is so happy tonight, General. So free of worry. How can I possibly tell her that the Tartars are beginning to massacre our people again?

*The Men solemnly watch the Women approach. The Czarina stops a distance away, listens to the music, smiles at her Guests. The Czar obviously loves her.*

CZAR ALEXANDER: Nerensky, find a courier immediately. The very best we have.

NERENSKY: Yes, Sire.

CZAR ALEXANDER: And we must prepare to mobilize the army.

*The Czarina joins her husband. Nerensky bows, then exits. Alexander kisses Catherine on the cheek, then arm-in-arm, the Monarchs descend the stairway.*

## 12. BALLROOM - INT/NIGHT

*The Orchestra stops playing. The Crowd is silent and respect-*
*ful. People bow as the Czar and Czarina pass. There is obvi-*
*ously great admiration for the Monarchs.*
    *Jolivet rises from his sofa, awe-struck.*

JOLIVET'S NARRATION [*voice over*]: "I had been in Mos-
        cow only a couple of days. My newspaper wanted
        me to write about this new, enlightened Russian
        court. If only my readers in Paris could have seen
        what I witnessed that night...the glory and maj-
        esty of the Czar and Czarina with their beloved
        subjects!"

*Jolivet bows deeply. The Monarchs sit on their thrones, then*
*Alexander signals the Musicians to resume playing.*
    *Dancing begins again. The Czar watches, but his eyes are*
*flecked with worry. But when Subjects approach him, he is*
*kind and attentive.*
    *Jolivet sketches the Monarchs. For a while he is sober.*
    *The Czarina whispers into the Czar's ear. They rise and*
*step to the dance floor. The People admire them and applaud.*
*Alexander and Catherine waltz, both moving gracefully.*

## 13. THE CZAR'S CHAMBERS - INT/NIGHT - LATER THAT EVENING

*A beautiful golden nightingale is perched in a gilded cage.*
*Princess Lara, a Little Girl in her nightgown, feeds seed to*
*the bird. She sings to the nightingale, but it remains silent.*

*The Czarina comes in. She, too, is dressed for bed.*

CZARINA CATHERINE: Lara, you should be in your bed.

PRINCESS LARA: I was saying good-night to Goldy. But he won't sing, Momma.

*The Czarina reaches into the cage and strokes the bird.*

PRINCESS LARA: I think he's sad.

CZARINA CATHERINE: What would he be sad about?

PRINCESS LARA: That he wasn't allowed to attend the ball.

*The Child pouts. Her Mother lifts her in her arms.*

CZARINA CATHERINE: There will be plenty of balls for you, my sweet.

*Czar Alexander enters. His Daughter runs to him.*

PRINCESS LARA: Father! I wanted to dance with you!

*The Czar twirls his Daughter around the room in an intimate waltz. The Girl is thrilled. She hugs her Father and rests her head on his shoulder.*
*The Czarina watches lovingly. She feeds more seed to the nightingale.*

CZARINA CATHERINE: It was kind of your brother to send us this beautiful creature.

*The Czar sets his Daughter down. She's a bit dizzy.*

CZARINA CATHERINE: We should go to Irkutsk and visit Theodore soon. He's returned from his mission to China, hasn't he, Alexander?

*The Czar becomes solemn at the mention of the Grand Duke.*

CZAR ALEXANDER: Yes, I believe he is back. If you remember, he got the nightingale in China. A rare breed, he was told.

PRINCESS LARA: Yes, oh please! Can we go visit the Grand Duke?

CZAR ALEXANDER: Perhaps. When the time is appropriate.

*The Czarina notices the Czar's worried expression.*

CZARINA CATHERINE: What's bothering you, my love?

CZAR ALEXANDER: Catherine, we have word…there may have been skirmishes in the frontier.

CZARINA CATHERINE: Is Theodore safe?

CZAR ALEXANDER: Yes. Nothing can harm the Grand
          Duke.

*But the Czarina sees uncertainty in her Husband's eyes,
and this frightens her. She turns to her Daughter.*

CZARINA CATHERINE: We are off to bed. Kiss your fa-
          ther goodnight, Lara.

*The Child does this, and the Czar embraces them both.*
*The Family stands together for a long moment, secure in
love and warmth and care. Then the Czarina and Princess
leave the Czar alone.*
*Alexander pours himself a large mug of brandy. He sits by
his fireplace and stares thoughtfully into the flames.*
*There's a loud knock on the door.*

CZAR ALEXANDER: Come!

*General Nerensky enters and bows. He carries a large map
under his arm.*

NERENSKY: Sire, the courier you asked for is on his way.
          He will be with us shortly.

CZAR ALEXANDER: Good. If you care for some brandy,
          General, you are welcome.

*The Czar indicates the table filled with liquors and glasses.*

NERENSKY: Thank you, Sire. It is always a pleasure to drink the royal brews.

*Both Men smile as Nerensky pours. They are obviously close friends.*

CZAR ALEXANDER: Tell me honestly, General. Is the Grand Duke Theodore in danger?

NERENSKY: Yes, Sire. Grave danger…if what we suspect is actually occurring.

*Nerensky lays his map out on a table near the fireplace. It depicts all of Russia, a huge area stretching from Europe to the Pacific. Vast plains, mountain ranges, rivers, lakes, deserts. Towns sprinkled throughout, connected by roads and portions of railroad track.*

NERENSKY: The last message by wire from Siberia was received from Omsk. Many towns in this central area are not answering us. It's obvious the Tartars are on the move, because this was their pattern before. Cut the towns off by telegraph, then attack when the people are unable to call for assistance.

CZAR ALEXANDER: Could it be…Feofar Khan?

NERENSKY: That's who we believe is behind this. We can't be sure how strong his numbers are, but the Horde is bound to have several thousand renegades. And I believe we should assume that his army grows in number every day.

CZAR ALEXANDER: Will this demon ever stop raiding our people?

NERENSKY: Not until we stop him.

CZAR ALEXANDER: Then Nerensky, we must make war in Siberia again.

NERENSKY: I believe it's possible to defeat the Tartars. We can transport troops into the frontier, and pick up other fighters as we move through the provinces.

*Czar Alexander stares at the map.*

CZAR ALEXANDER: I worry now that perhaps Colonel Zurevno has plans to join Feofar Khan. At his trial, you must remember what he said.

NERENSKY: It was treasonous. We should have put the man to death on the spot.

CZAR ALEXANDER: He said: 'Alexander, if you were as strong a ruler as the great Khan, I would not have felt the need to grasp control from you. I would have gladly bathed in your bloody glory.'

NERENSKY: Pure abomination!

CZAR ALEXANDER: If Zurevno joins Khan, then we will
      have some trouble. He was a competent officer, a
      fine leader in battle. He knows our strategies as
      well as any other soldier.

NERENSKY: We must assume that is his plan.

*The Czar goes to the nightingale, strokes its golden feathers.*

CZAR ALEXANDER: Usually this creature sings all night.
      But for some reason it is silent this evening.
      Strange…it has such a wonderful voice….

*General Nerensky pours himself another drink and continues to study his map.*

CZAR ALEXANDER: General, this courier…do you know
      the soldier personally?

NERENSKY: Only by reputation. My staff recommends
      him highly. He is a young man who knows the
      territory well. Also, he's been decorated for valor
      in battle on several occasions.

CZAR ALEXANDER: His name?

NERENSKY: Lieutenant Michael Strogoff.

## 14. PALACE BALLROOM - INT/NIGHT -
   AT THIS SAME TIME

*All the Guests have gone except Jolivet. He is drunk and half-asleep on the couch. Maids clean the room. One approaches him, shakes him on the shoulder. His eyes open.*

MAID: Sir? May I help you find your way home?

JOLIVET: I am a guest of the Czar. I am staying in a room
            right here in the Palace. I can certainly find my
            own way, thank you.

*The Maid leaves, smirking at him. She whispers to the other Maids and they smile in fun at Jolivet.*
*The Journalist stands, straightens his rumpled coat, walks drunkenly out into the hallway. Then he falls to the floor, hitting his head.*
*From Jolivet's point-of-view: two polished boots approach, the scarlet uniform of the Imperial Guard. Jolivet is helped to his feet, and he looks into the handsome young face of Michael Strogoff.*

STROGOFF: You are not well, friend.

JOLIVET: I'll be fine. Can you find me a chair?

*Michael leads Jolivet across the floor to a place near the stairway. Jolivet sits. Michael goes to a Maid, returns with a glass of water for the Journalist, who is rubbing his head.*

JOLIVET: Thank you, but I prefer wine. 'Fine wine is the blood of the soul.' Who said that? I can't remember. A French poet, certainly.

STROGOFF: I must go. Good evening. And please be careful.

*Michael salutes Jolivet, then continues up the stairway. Jolivet returns the salute to his back, mocking but friendly.*

JOLIVET'S NARRATION [*voice-over*]: "I first met Michael Strogoff in a rather absurd situation, but I was struck by his demeanor. He seemed the perfect soldier, but there was a kindness to him where in others you sometimes find only arrogance. I had no way of knowing at the time what the fellow was about to endure - what he and I would endure together. But Fate has a way of marking certain men…"

## 15. THE CZAR'S CHAMBER, OUTER DOOR - INT/NIGHT - MOMENTS LATER

*Two large Cossacks stand guard, also Major Torlov. Michael salutes the Major, their eyes lock with familiarity.*

TORLOV: Lieutenant, please leave all your weapons on this table.

STROGOFF: Yes, Sir.

*Michael removes his saber. He takes his pistol from his belt. He takes a large bear-knife from his tunic. He takes a sharp dagger from his hat. Then finally, a smaller pistol from his boot.*

*As he is stooped, fixing his pants back into the boot, he whispers to Torlov intimately.*

STROGOFF: Karl, what is this about?

TORLOV: It is a very important mission, Michael. You're going back to Siberia.

STROGOFF: Back home? Are you sure?

TORLOV: Yes. Now hurry! General Nerensky is impatient.

*Michael stands back up, straightens his tunic. Torlov resumes his normal command voice, for the sake of the Guards.*

TORLOV: Lieutenant, have you ever been in His Majesty's presence before?

STROGOFF: No, Sir.

TORLOV: Well, try to be…dignified.

STROGOFF: Yes, Sir.

*Torlov knocks loudly on the door.*

NERENSKY [*voice-over*]: Enter!

*The Two Officers go through the door. When they pass, the Guards look at each other with amusement.*

## 16. THE CZAR'S CHAMBER - INT/NIGHT

*Torlov and Strogoff enter. They bow and salute. The General and the Czar watch them solemnly.*

TORLOV: I have brought the courier. Lieutenant Michael Strogoff.

NERENSKY: Thank you, Major. You may stay.

*Torlov moves to the side so Michael can stand alone before his Superiors.*

CZAR ALEXANDER: Have you been told anything about this mission?

STROGOFF: No, Sire.

*Torlov keeps his eyes straight ahead but nervously swallows. No one notices.*

CZAR ALEXANDER: You must not mention this meeting to anyone. We must have absolute secrecy.

STROGOFF: Yes, Sire.

*The Czar keeps his eyes on Michael, but with a gesture defers to General Nerensky.*

NERENSKY: Strogoff, I'm sure that you're aware of the rumours of a possible Tartar uprising in the frontier.

STROGOFF: The men in the barracks talk of little else these days.

NERENSKY: We now believe this to be genuine fact.

*Michael nods solemnly.*

CZAR ALEXANDER: Where were you raised, Strogoff?

STROGOFF: Siberia, Sire. Near Omsk.

CZAR ALEXANDER: Well. You may be the perfect man for our needs.

*Torlov stares at the liquor table, craving a drink.*

CZAR ALEXANDER: Do you have family, Strogoff?

STROGOFF: Just my old mother. She still lives in Omsk. Is she in danger, Sire?

*The General and Czar glance at each other. Michael notices.*

CZAR ALEXANDER: We're not sure, Lieutenant. Possibly there is danger near that town. But at present we can't be sure how expansive this insurrection is. It may be simply a renegade army...sporadic raids here and there ...

STROGOFF: Not if Feofar Khan is involved!

*The room becomes tense with Michael's interruption, and knowledge.*

STROGOFF: Forgive me for speaking out, Sire.

CZAR ALEXANDER: No. I want to hear what you have to say. What do you know of the Khan?

STROGOFF: Sire, he's a devil living in the flesh of a man. What his men do to prisoners...men and women...children! I've seen it with my own eyes.

CZAR ALEXANDER: When was this? Khan has been in exile for many years. You have not fought him.

STROGOFF: Sire, my father was a bear-hunter. When I was young, we went on a hunt together. We were after a big white, those bears that only live in Siberia. The ones with teeth almost half a foot long. I got my first bear on that hunt. Killed the beast with spear first, then bullet. The old way, the tradition. I skinned him myself. I was proud. My father and I were on our way home, using a trail through the forest to save time. We had done our work well. Suddenly we saw a horrible thing. In a clearing, bodies were hanging upside down from trees. They'd had their eyes cut out, their tongues severed…other parts of their bodies slashed off. Fires had been lit under them. The coals were still warm. Two men, a woman, three little children. The ants and bugs had already started to feast….

*The Men are silent, their faces tightened in disgust and rage.*

STROGOFF: Later, the Tartars attacked our village. But they were beaten back by Cossack strength.

*The Czar stares thoughtfully at the Soldier.*

CZAR ALEXANDER: Lieutenant, you may have something to drink, if you'd like. Major?

*Torlov gratefully goes to the liquor table, pours a couple of mugs of brandy and hands one to Michael.*

NERENSKY: Lieutenant, what do you know about Colonel Zurevno?

STROGOFF: May he burn in Hell, Sir. Along with the Khan.

NERENSKY: Zurevno may be joining forces with the Tartars.

STROGOFF: I don't understand. Isn't the man to be executed?

NERENSKY: Zurevno escaped this very night. He murdered a Bishop of the Church, assumed the priest's identity, and rode away.

STROGOFF: I never met Colonel Zurevno. I never set eyes on the man. But he's a traitor as sure as I know anything!

*The Czar stands and goes to his desk. The Soldiers are silent and respectful, as the Monarch seems self-absorbed. Michael Strogoff studies the map intently.*

*Alexander takes up his quill pen and begins to write, a distinctive script.*

THE CZAR'S LETTER [*voice-over*]: "To the Grand Duke Theodore. Dear Brother, this courier, Michael Strogoff, bears news of the gravest nature. As you know, the Tartar Horde is growing in strength, and soon may invade your territory. I have no doubt you can hold Irkutsk until we are able to send Imperial troops to aid in your defence. But I implore you, my brother, you must be careful of the traitor Colonel Victor Zurevno. While you were away in China, this vile turncoat led an officer's revolt at the Palace. He has unfortunately escaped, and may attempt to enter your court incognito. He is a spy and a murderer, known to travel in disguise. Beware of him!

May God be with you, Brother. We must stand for Mother Russia as never before. Czar Alexander."

*The Czar signals Michael to join him at the desk.*

CZAR ALEXANDER: Lieutenant, it is not the usual procedure, as you know, for a courier to read a personal dispatch from his Czar. But under these unique circumstances I've decided to amend this policy. Read this message before I seal it. I want you to know its contents in case some emergency occurs. If so, you're to dispose of the paper.

*Michael takes the letter and reads it carefully.*

CZAR ALEXANDER: Do you understand?

STROGOFF: Yes, Sire.

*The Czar dips his Imperial ring in ink, stamps the Imperial crest below his name, folds the letter, pours sealing wax, presses the ring into it, again the crest.*
*He hands the letter to Michael.*
*The Courier opens his tunic and removes an oil-skin packet cut perfectly to fit dispatches. His necklace is suddenly revealed, a long sharp bear-tooth. It catches the Czar's eye.*

CZAR ALEXANDER: What is that, Lieutenant?

STROGOFF: A trophy, Sire. From a great white. My last hunt before joining the army.

*The Courier quickly sticks the packet into his tunic and buttons up, embarrassed.*

CZAR ALEXANDER: You will not reveal your mission to anyone. And no one must know who you really are.

STROGOFF: Yes, Sire.

CZAR ALEXANDER: Do you draw luck from that trophy you wear?

STROGOFF: It's said that if you eat of the beast, you become like the beast. You take its power into yourself.

*The Czar is impressed.*

CZAR ALEXANDER: I hope what you say is true. You have a difficult journey ahead. But until we crush the renegade Hordes, many demands will be made of us all….

STROGOFF: Thank you for trusting me, Sire.

*Michael bows.*

CZAR ALEXANDER: You have our blessings.

*Michael turns, salutes the General, and leaves the chamber. Major Torlov follows him out.*
*Czar Alexander is weary. He strokes the nightingale again,*

*then is about to cover the cage with a silk scarf when the bird sings.*

*The Czar smiles.*

CZAR ALEXANDER: Now you sing for us, little one.

*The General wraps his map and prepares to leave.*

CZAR ALEXANDER: General, have we sent this man on
        a futile mission tonight?

NERENSKY: It's possible that he might get through.

CZAR ALEXANDER: I fear we have some hard times
        ahead, old friend.

NERENSKY: I fear it, also, Sire.

*Nerensky exits, leaving his Czar alone to brood by the fire.*


## 17. THE PRINCESS'S BEDROOM - INT/NIGHT

*Czarina Catherine and Princess Lara on their knees saying
their evening prayers. Their eyes lift to the Orthodox Crucifix
on the wall.*

*Catherine helps Lara into bed. She tucks the blankets and
silk quilt around the Child. She starts to blow out the lamp—*

PRINCESS LARA: Momma, please tell me a story.

CZARINA CATHERINE: I am very tired, Lara. Tomorrow night I'll—

PRINCESS LARA: Please! I couldn't go to the ball tonight. And now nobody will even tell me a story!

CZARINA CATHERINE: All right, little girl. Only one, and it will be very short.

*The Girl snuggles close to her Mother.*

CZARINA CATHERINE: Once there was a young Princess—

PRINCESS LARA: Is this about me?

CZARINA CATHERINE: No, Lara. Now close your eyes.

PRINCESS LARA: I hope you put a bird in this story.

*Catherine smiles, then kisses her Daughter's forehead. Lara closes her eyes to listen.*

CZARINA CATHERINE: Once there was a young Princess. She lived in the Land of Snow. The Princess liked to paint beautiful pictures of birds and animals. But she was disenchanted and lonely, because she was not allowed to leave her tower. The Dark Spirits kept her prisoner there. One night she looked out her window, praying to the full moon for freedom. Suddenly an Ice Maiden appeared out of the sky. The Ice Maiden had been concerned for the Princess, and she had heard the Princess weeping in her heart. 'Why are you so sad?' asked the Ice Maiden. 'I'm sad because I want to escape from this tower', said the Princess. The Ice Maiden smiled knowingly, then she whispered a secret into the Princess's ear. The Princess almost wept with happiness, but then suddenly the Ice Maiden disappeared back into the sky. For the next few weeks, the Princess worked very hard on a new painting. It filled a huge canvas that covered an entire wall. The picture was of a gigantic Firebird, as red and warm and bright as the sun the Princess only vaguely remembered… since in the Land of Snow it was always white and blue and dark. On the next full moon, the Princess did exactly what the Ice Maiden told her. She prayed to the moon so strongly that her heart almost broke. But the Spirits of Light heard her prayer. And the giant Firebird she had painted came alive! The huge wings caused a great fiery wind to blow the roof from the tower. The Firebird had a kind face, and he loved his creator, the Princess. So he swept her onto his back, and he flew away with her into the sky. The Princess laughed for the very first time, and it echoed across the snow. She was now free from the Dark Spirits forever. The Firebird took her to the Land of Sun she had always dreamed about. And there the Princess lived in a forest filled with many friendly animals that she brought to life herself with her fine paintings.

*Princess Lara has fallen asleep, but there's a smile of contentment on her face. The Czarina blows out the lamp.*

## 18. OFFICER'S QUARTERS - INT/NIGHT

*Before a mirror, Michael Strogoff changes from his uniform into the clothes of a regular citizen. Major Torlov briefs him.*

TORLOV: You will travel under the name of "Nicholas Korpanoff." A merchant…let's say a horse trader. Nicholas Korpanoff is on his way to his home in Irkutsk. Here are his papers, and also a special pass.

*Torlov places the documents on a table. The pass is adorned by the Czar's official crest.*

TORLOV: The pass allows you to take horses from any post-station. But only do this in an emergency. You must not draw attention to yourself as belonging to the Government.

*The Major places a leather pouch beside the documents.*

TORLOV: And here is plenty of money. Just be careful you don't drink it all away…or spend it on women.

*Michael smiles subtly at the joke. But it's obvious his mind is already far away on his mission. He finishes dressing, then begins to clean his pistol and sharpen his bear-knife.*

TORLOV: You will take the train to Novgorod this morning, then go by steamboat to Perm. From then
on, how you get across the mountains and to
Irkutsk is your own business.

*Torlov is impressed by how Michael handles his weapons.*

TORLOV: You must watch out for yourself, Michael. These
Tartars are not bears. They are much more dangerous.

*Michael is ready to go. He lifts his small carpetbag.*

TORLOV: My orders are to escort you to the station and
see that you get on the train.

STROGOFF: You're a fine friend, Karl.


## 19. MOSCOW STATION - EXT/DAWN

*The sky is gray, and the sun begins to rise. Torlov is asleep on
a bench beside Michael, but the Courier is wide awake and
alert.*

*He watches intently as the new sun's rays streak across the
hills, the light glistening in his eyes.*

*From the distant track, the train is coming. The station is
nearly empty of Passengers, so there are few to greet it.*

*Michael shakes Torlov by the shoulder.*

STROGOFF: Karl.

*Michael stands, stretches his legs. The chilly air enlivens him. Torlov sits up groggily.*

*The train pulls into the station. Its brakes squeal, sparks fly on the rails. Steam gushes forth.*

*The Men embrace silently. Then Michael walks to his train alone.*

∽

## 20. THE COUNTRYSIDE, ON THE RAILROAD - EXT/DAY

MONTAGE: *Of landscape as the train moves across the territory. Fields of green grass, large brown hills, forests of tall trees. A sparkling river drenched in sun.*

*A herd of reindeer leap across the track in front of the locomotive. The shrill whistle blows.*

## 21. THE TRAIN - INT/DAY

*Through the window of the car, Michael watches the reindeer. He smiles at their beauty and grace. The country seems to rush by his eyes.*

*A farm house, with a huge bear-skin being stretched between two trees. An Old Man works on it. His Young Son waves at the passing train. Michael smiles to himself, touches the bear-tooth necklace under his white starched shirt.*

*Other Passengers in the car: A well-dressed Merchant reading a book…a Young Man and his Wife, she pregnant, gazing out at the exquisite land…an Old Cossack smoking his pipe.*

*Beyond them, filling the rest of the car, a Troop of Soldiers. They are all young, boisterous, care free. All except for their Captain, who solemnly studies a map.*

*Michael recognizes the Man and whispers his name secretly.*

STROGOFF: Ravski!

*Michael turns his head full to the window, out of Ravski's view. But he can watch the Captain's reflection in the glass. Ravski is preoccupied, so after a few moments Michael rests easy.*

*The sun beats on Michael's face, making a double-reflection of him in the window. The sun light tires his eyes, so he closes them to try to rest.*

ະ

## 22. A WATER STATION, DOWN THE LINE - EXT/DAY

*Through his office window, the Station Master sees Someone riding up on a horse ready to collapse. It looks like a Priest in trouble. He walks onto the platform and stares against the sun.*

*Zurevno walks the horse across the tracks. His face is grimy and sun-burnt under the Bishop's hood. He ties the horse to a hitching post and sits on a bench, his eyes staring at the Station Master. The Man bows to the "Bishop".*

ZUREVNO: I'd like some water.

STATION MASTER: Yes, Father. Right away.

*The Man runs back into his office, then immediately returns with a large mug of water. Zurevno gulps it down.*

*The Station Master stares at the horse, which has fallen to the ground. He's displeased seeing the animal run so hard.*

ZUREVNO: Do you have food?

STATION MASTER: Yes.

*The Man goes back to his office. Zurevno looks around, notices the two fresh horses prancing in the corral. There is also a wagon.*

*The Station Master returns with a wooden tray laden with food: A loaf of bread, cheese, a goblet of wine, an apple.*

STATION MASTER: Please accept this, Father.

*Zurevno nods and digs in.*

STATION MASTER: You have traveled far?

ZUREVNO: Yes.

STATION MASTER: From Moscow?

*Zurevno nods his head and chews.*

STATION MASTER: May I ask your destination, Father?

ZUREVNO: Novgorod.

STATION MASTER: You're in luck. The train to Novgorod
    will be along later today.

*Zurevno drains the wine, which the Station Master finds
a bit odd.*

ZUREVNO: I would like to buy a horse. There is Church
    business that will not wait.

STATION MASTER: I'm very sorry, Father. There are no
    more animals here.

*Zurevno stares at the two in the corral. The Station Master sees him looking.*

STATION MASTER: Those are not for sale. They belong
    to the Station.

*Suddenly, the "Bishop's" horse coughs, and blood spills from
its mouth. The Station Master is appalled.*

STATION MASTER: I must do something for him! Do I
    have your permission, Father?

*Zurevno waves his arm nonchalantly. The Station Master
again runs into his office, this time returning with a rifle. He
goes to the horse, unties it from the hitching-post, and leads
the sick animal away from the tracks.*
    *Zurevno watches with amusement, but he never stops eating.*
    *The "Bishop's" horse collapses again and won't rise. The*

*Man places the rifle to its temple and fires, killing the horse instantly.*

*He sadly walks back toward Zurevno.*

STATION MASTER: Forgive me for saying this, Father...but it was cruel the way you treated him. We must show mercy to beasts who are below us—

*Zurevno pulls out his pistol and fires. The Station Master falls to the dust, dead.*

*Zurevno turns the body over, takes the Man's watch, his money, his rifle. He goes into the office, takes the money-box from underneath the counter, also, a water flask.*

*At the corral, he saddles one of the horses, then slips a halter and long reins over the other.*

*He mounts the horse, leads the second. He rides away in the general direction the railroad tracks are heading.*

∽

## 23. THE TRAIN - INT/DAY - LATER

*Michael awakens to lively conversation from the Passengers.*

MERCHANT: Yes, the Fair in Novgorod promises to be quite an exciting event. I plan to have my own booth to sell my wares.

YOUNG HUSBAND: Marie and I plan to live there permanently. We've just been married.

*The Young Wife smiles, wrapping her shawl tighter to warm her large belly.*

MERCHANT: Congratulations. I'm Yosha Kemel. I sell a fine collection of jewelry. Broaches, watches, bracelets, necklaces, combs. Wedding rings?

*The Young Wife shows him hers.*

YOUNG WIFE: I would never sell this—it's from Jonathan—but what value would you place on the ring, Mr. Kemel?

*The Merchant holds her hand and studies the ring.*

MERCHANT: This is an authentic diamond?

*The Couple look at each other amusingly. Kemel takes out his jeweler's glass, sticks it in his eye, examines the ring. Then the Couple starts to laugh, as the Merchant also smiles.*

MERCHANT: You young people, you had me interested! That is no diamond, but an exquisite crystal. Certainly valuable.

YOUNG WIFE: You can have good luck with a crystal stone. A happy future!

YOUNG HUSBAND: That ring was in my family for years.

MERCHANT: Let me show you something.

*He opens his large case of goods and removes an ivory comb. He hands it to the Wife.*

MERCHANT: This is my present, for your new marriage and your coming family.

YOUNG WIFE: Oh, it's beautiful. But no, I can't accept.

YOUNG HUSBAND: No, thank you, Mr. Kemel.

MERCHANT: Nonsense! My gift! A lovely girl needs lovely things.

*The Young Woman takes the comb. She immediately starts to use it on her long hair. The Merchant stares at her too warmly. The Husband tries to dispel this lecherous attention.*

HUSBAND: I'm a school teacher. Novgorod will be my new post.

MERCHANT: You hope to educate the country children. Maybe it's possible.

*Michael's face stiffens at this offense. But the Old Cossack suddenly speaks through his cloud of pipe smoke—*

OLD COSSACK: When the Tartars come, the only education worth a damn will be knowledge of the gun and sword.

*Everyone is shocked by this statement. Except Michael.*

OLD COSSACK: They'll just love that pretty hair of yours,
little lady.

HUSBAND: I don't appreciate you talking like this to my
wife!

*The Cossack laughs. There is tension. The Young Woman
stops combing her hair, embarrassed. Michael watches everyone silently.*

MERCHANT: I was led to believe the Tartars all live in
Tibet now. And they're just a pitiful tribe of renegades wasting away…who can't even feed their
children.

*The Old Cossack stretches his leg, and it's revealed to be
wooden. Carved on it are intricate designs, exotic symbols.*

OLD COSSACK: I don't know what they feed their children, but a pack of their wolf-hounds once got a
big chunk of me for supper.

*Everyone pales and seems disturbed, yet fascinated.*

OLD COSSACK: Ten years ago when the Khan tried to
invade us, I fought the bastard. I killed my share
of Heathens. But one battle I got unlucky. I got
shot, fell off my horse, and the Horde trampled
me. My leg just got torn right off. A pack of wolf-
hounds ran in and made off with it like a turkey
for the Holy Day.

*The People are uncomfortable, but the Old Cossack smiles.*

OLD COSSACK: Anybody got an idea what all these soldiers are doing on this train? What do you think, young fellow?

*He looks at Michael, who shrugs as if ignorant. But the Young Husband challenges him—*

HUSBAND: I've heard rumors, but that's all it is! Gossip. People trying to scare people. How could you know what is going on, Old Man?

*The Old Cossack just stares silently, smiling and quietly refilling his pipe as if the conversation is ended.*
*The shrill train whistle and squealing brakes shatter the tension.*
*Michael walks out on the railing. Up ahead is the water station. Suddenly he turns, and behind him is Jolivet, the French Journalist. Michael ducks past him quickly.*
*Jolivet nods to Michael, but the Courier pretends not to know him. He disappears to the other side of the train.*

JOLIVET'S NARRATION [*voice-over*]: "I recognized him immediately, yet for some strange reason he avoided my eyes. He was no longer in uniform, but I was sure this was the same young soldier who had kindly assisted me at the Czar's ball. I would have gone after him, but suddenly the train screeched to a halt…and the most horrible sight took my full attention."

*The Passengers see the dead horse and the dead Station Master, the corpses hideously feasted upon by vultures.*

## 24. THE WATER STATION - EXT/DAY

*Captain Ravski leaps angrily from the train. With his rifle he shoots a vulture from the Station Master's body, and this scatters the other birds.*

*Michael watches discretely from a corner compartment.*

*At Ravski's command, the Soldiers surround the station. With rifles at the ready, they search…but find nothing.*

*The train Engineer orders the locomotive serviced, so the Workers set about the task. Water is let loose from the tower into the chute that leads to the train. Coal from the large shed is loaded on.*

*Passengers disembark to stretch their legs. The Young Wife is horrified at the sight of such death and rot. The Merchant is nearly sick, his eyes wide with fear. But the Old Cossack looks on coldly. The Young Husband approaches him, as if to ask something, but changes his mind.*

*Captain Ravski investigates the office. Then he dictates a telegraph message that a Young Soldier sends. The Journalist Jolivet watches them through the window, sitting on the bench outside and sketching the scene of death.*

JOLIVET'S NARRATION [*voice-over*]: "There had been rumors of a possible conflict on the frontier, which is why I decided to accompany Captain Ravski's troop. But could this tragedy we found have been caused by Tartar renegades, this close to Moscow? I doubted it. This is such exquisite country. The people are loyal to each other, and to the Czar. But before me lay a mystery…"

*Michael Strogoff quietly gets off the train at the far end, away from Ravski and Jolivet. He pretends to stretch his legs and to be simply curious. He makes his way to the dead horse.*

*Two Soldiers guard the carcass. Michael takes out his handkerchief and covers his mouth as if he's sick.*

SOLDIER #1: Bad meat, sir.

SOLDIER #2: Very bad.

*They laugh at Michael's apparent weakness. Then one Soldier becomes serious.*

SOLDIER #2: See that blood? And how beaten he was? Somebody rode this animal to his end.

*Michael suddenly sees something on the horse's flank: a brand. The Orthodox Cross, symbol of the Church's special stable.*

*The land around him is vast. Keeping his back toward the crowd, Michael pulls a spy-glass from his coat. He studies the terrain carefully. He sees no rider, but horse tracks lead along the railroad line ahead.*

## 25. THE TRAIN - INT/NIGHT - LATER

*Most of the Passengers sleep. The Old Cossack snores…the Merchant clutches his product case and dreams fitfully…the Wife lays with her head in her Husband's lap, and he strokes her hair. But Michael Strogoff is wide awake.*

*Some of the Soldiers are, also. One of them plays his violin, and there is singing. A moody, romantic Warrior's lament.*

*Michael listens with pleasure.*

*Outside his window, the land is dark. But gradually, as the train comes around a hill…the lights of Novgorod.*

∽

## 26. NOVGOROD STATION - EXT/NIGHT

*The train pulls in. Passengers disembark, going separate directions. The Soldiers led by Ravski march off in precise order. Jolivet follows wearily behind.*

*Michael waits until the platform is clear, then leaves the train. He hurries along, careful to appear inconspicuous.*

## 27. THE CITY STREETS - EXT/NIGHT

*Michael walks through the town. People mill about in a festive mood. He passes a tavern, looks in the window. The Crowd is lively.*

*A Woman stumbles out the door, sees him, grabs his arm.*

WOMAN: Come in, pretty one. Buy me a rum?

STROGOFF: No, thank you. I have business.

WOMAN: Well, pretty one, I am hurt. But be careful...
someone will get that heart of yours!

*The Woman laughs, as does Michael. She goes back into
the tavern and Michael continues on.*

*The dark street leads down to the docks, and the many
boats there.*

## 28. THE HARBOR - EXT/NIGHT

*The Steamboat 'Caucasus' stands in the water. Sailors finish
various jobs: cleaning the deck, painting the hull, patching
the chimney. From across the dock, Michael calls to one of the
Men.*

STROGOFF: Where can I find your Captain?

*The Sailor points to a large stack of crates and boxes at the
far side of the dock. Michael walks over. The Captain is checking inventory.*

STROGOFF: Are you the man in charge?

CAPTAIN: Who might you be?

STROGOFF: My name is Nicholas Korpanoff. A message
was sent from Moscow reserving passage for me
on your boat. To Perm.

*The Captain flips through his papers.*

CAPTAIN: Yes, you're on the list.

STROGOFF: Are we sailing this evening?

CAPTAIN: Not tonight. Tomorrow, Mr. Korpanoff. Noon
at the earliest.

*Michael is disturbed by this delay.*

STROGOFF: Problems, Captain?

CAPTAIN: With this Fair going on, I can't get enough
workers. So my Seamen have to do more than
their normal share. And my second officer ran off
with a gypsy girl today. So as you see, tonight I'm
a clerk. We will be lucky if we have this cargo
loaded by dawn!

*Michael nods, understanding the Captain's frustration.*

STROGOFF: I must get there soon.

CAPTAIN: What is your business, sir?

STROGOFF: I trade in horses.

CAPTAIN: Well, Perm is the place to go for that.

*The Captain goes back to his work, ignoring Michael.*

## 29. CITY STREETS - EXT/NIGHT

*Michael wanders, looking for a particular building. The Crowd is thick and festive, but Michael is solemn.*

*At a far corner, he stops. The sign on the building says 'Inn of the Blue Rose'. The design is the flower sprouting from snow.*

## 30. 'INN OF THE BLUE ROSE' - INT/NIGHT

*It's warm inside, a fire blazes at the hearth. A few People eat in a dining room. Michael goes to the front counter, a Matron is there.*

STROGOFF: Do you still have room tonight?

MATRON: Only one left.

*Michael writes 'Nicholas Korpanoff' in the ledger and hands her some money.*

MATRON: Come this way.

*They move up the stairway, just as a Young Woman is walking down. She is beautiful with long blond hair. This is Nadia, and Michael can't take his eyes from her. Nadia sits alone in the dining room, self-absorbed.*

*Michael just stares. Her light eyes, smooth skin. She carries a book as if to read, but she can't because a letter in her hand has all her thoughts.*

*Suddenly, Nadia stares up at Michael. Their eyes lock intensely. Michael sees Nadia is close to weeping.*

*The Matron coughs impatiently.*

MATRON: Sir?

STROGOFF: Oh, yes.

*They move back up the stairs. Michael looks down again, but Nadia has looked away…back to her letter.*

## 31. MICHAEL'S ROOM - INT/NIGHT - MOMENTS LATER

*It's small, spare but adequate. Michael stares out the window through his spy-glass: campfires where the fair is being set up. People drinking, dancing spontaneously near the flames. Gypsy music.*

*He takes out the pouch containing the Czar's dispatch. He holds it delicately, as if it's alive. He places it under the rug, but this doesn't seem right, so he sticks it under his pillow.*

*He sits on the bed and rubs his weary eyes. But he's anxious. He sticks the dispatch back in his coat. Then he checks himself in the mirror and leaves the room.*

## 32. DOWNSTAIRS - INT/NIGHT

*Michael looks around for Nadia, but her table is now empty. This saddens him. He slowly walks back upstairs.*

## 33. MICHAEL'S ROOM - INT/NIGHT

*He lays on the bed, fully clothed. He turns down the lamp and tries to rest, but his eyes remain open, staring at the ceiling.*

## 34. THE FAIRGROUNDS - EXT/NIGHT

*The last of the tents go up. Wild beasts settle in their cages. People huddle at campfires. Cossacks ride through the area on patrol.*

## 35. GYPSY TENT - INT/NIGHT

*Sangarre, a beautiful Gypsy Woman, bathes at her water bowl. Her dark hair is cut short like a man's. She's naked except for the jeweled dagger hanging between her breasts.*

*She sponges herself, water rolling down her fine skin. She doesn't notice the hand that slowly opens her tent's rear-flap.*

*Sangarre towels off. But suddenly, in her mirror, she sees the Intruder. She spins around expertly, her dagger ready for the fight.*

*The Intruder laughs deeply and removes his dark hood. It is Zurevno.*

SANGARRE: Victor!

ZUREVNO: My love.

SANGARRE: Are you a ghost?

*Zurevno silently stares at her, then smiles. Sangarre sees
how dirty and tired he is.*
*He reaches for her. She resists, but not forcefully.*

ZUREVNO: I've traveled a very long way.

*They kiss passionately.*

SANGARRE: I knew they couldn't hold you.

*Sangarre breaks away and secures the tent flap. Just then
the Cossacks ride by outside. Zurevno ducks down in fear.*

SANGARRE: You are safe here. The Russians don't bother
        anyone unless they make very bad trouble.

*Zurevno takes a long drink from Sangarre's bottle of rum.
The Woman playfully sniffs the air.*

SANGARRE: I should bathe you —Father!

*Zurevno reaches for her again, but she moves away.*

SANGARRE: No! You are a priest now, Victor. It is not
        right for a priest to—

*He holds her tight, kisses her breasts. He slips the dagger
from her neck and kisses her there, then her lips.*

*They lay on the pillows. She helps him off with his filthy robe and shirt. She's shocked to see long dark scars covering his back, wounds from a flogging.*

SANGARRE: They did this to you?

*Zurevno is grim, remembering.*

ZUREVNO: One of the many favors I owe his Imperial
     Majesty!

*Sangarre pours oil on her fingers and rubs it into his scars…this gradually leading to passionate love-making.*


## 36. THE TENT - INT/NIGHT - AFTERWARD

*Sangarre watches Zurevno sleep. She puts on her robe, bunches up his grimy clothes, carries them outside and throws them onto the campfire. They burn.*

*Sitting on a stump nearby is Toma, a large Bohemian. He looks at Sangarre while sharpening his knife. They obviously know each other well. She indicates that Zurevno is sleeping by placing her hands beneath her cheek. Toma nods and keeps watching, a fine Sentinel.*

*Back in the tent the Woman settles down beside the Colonel. Her fingers lovingly trace his scars again.*

༄

## 37. THE FAIR - EXT/DAY

*Michael wanders through the crowded tents, periodically checking his pocket watch. He looks toward the harbor anxiously, but much excitement surrounds him.*

*There are many booths. Merchants sell everything: jewelry, clothes, livestock, rare perfumes and medicines, exotic foods. Asians, Russians, all mingle together. There are wild acts: Fire-eaters, Sword-swallowers, Acrobats, Musicians, Dancers. A tattooed Giant walks around with a Midget on his shoulders.*

*At a medicine booth, something strange catches Michael's eye: the fetus of Siamese Twins joined at the spine, floating in a large jar. The Chinese Merchant smiles.*

CHINESE MERCHANT: You want to touch?

STROGOFF: No.

CHINESE MERCHANT: I make you good price. Trade
          for your watch and diamond ring.

STROGOFF: I don't have a diamond ring.

CHINESE MERCHANT: Could you get one?

*Michael shakes his head and moves on. Suddenly he sees Nadia at a far booth. She appears to be bargaining for a silk scarf, but in frustration she returns it to the Seamstress and leaves.*

*Michael hurries after her, but stops at the booth and picks up the scarf. It is colorful with wild birds in flight.*

STROGOFF: I want this.

*He tosses plenty of coins to the Seamstress, then quickly runs after Nadia, but he can't find her. She's lost in the crowd somewhere. Michael gently folds the scarf away in his coat.*

*A loud roar gets his attention. In a huge cage is a great white bear, a chain around his neck held by the Trainer. He cracks a whip and the bear sits on command. Children in the crowd are fascinated. Michael stares sadly at the beast being tamed.*

*Through the bars, on the other side of the cage, Michael's eyes meet Jolivet's. The Journalist looks up from his sketching of the animal, and nods in recognition. Michael quickly turns his back and hurries away.*

JOLIVET'S NARRATION [*voice-over*]: "It seemed like all the people of all the races on earth had come to this fair. I had never experienced anything like it in my life. It was so wild and colorful. So exotic and splendid to the eye. If my friends in Paris had been with me, what would they have thought? Perhaps that Russia was the meeting place of the world, her very air filled with pleasure and good-will!"

*At a food tent, Michael buys a bowl of rice with chicken. He eats as he walks, stopping near a group of Acrobats. They clown as they build human pyramids, then pretend to fall stupidly, yet displaying great expertise. Children laugh and clap their hands.*

*Music from a Gypsy tent. A Belly-Dancer enters. People*

*are enthralled by her sensuality, especially the Men. A jewel like a glimmering eye pulsates from her navel. A Drummer plays a tabla, his rhythm building in wild crescendo. The Crowd claps and stomps their feet. The Dancer smiles, shimmies, her flesh glistens with sweat—*

*Suddenly a loud commotion drowns out the music. The Russian Troops led by Captain Ravski gallop their horses past tents and booths. People scatter to get out of the way. Mothers grab up their Children. Animals are spooked and must be held.*

*It's a great disturbance, but Ravski yells for order.*

RAVSKI: Silence! Everyone be silent!

*But the Crowd will not quiet down. Ravski nods to his Troops, and they fire rifles into the air. The Crowd is stunned, Ravski screams out.*

RAVSKI: I order you to be silent!

*The Crowd finally settles, from fear and from awe of the Captain. He pulls out an official paper and reads:*

RAVSKI: "By order of the Czar, this fair is hereby closed. All people of Asian or other questionable blood must vacate Novgorod immediately!"

*People are confused. Troops begin to single out Asians and try to steer them from the grounds. There is shouting, scuffling. Fights break out. People who were once friendly now look at each other with suspicion. There is cursing and fear.*

*Tents go down. People pack their goods. Animals are herded. Some Asians protest. Soldiers draw their swords. They're assaulted by rocks thrown by some of the Asians. The Soldiers charge into a Group. People fall bleeding. The Crowd is shaken to near-riot proportions.*

*Most of the White Merchants make their way toward either the central city, or the harbor.*

*Michael searches for Nadia in the turmoil, but she's nowhere to be seen.*

*Jolivet is solemn amidst the chaos he witnesses.*

JOLIVET'S NARRATION [*voice-over*]: "It broke my heart to see such a joyous event come to such a disturbing end. Why had the Czar ordered this evacuation? Perhaps the rumors of war were based on truth. But why be so afraid of all these people just because some of their race had revolted?"

*A Soldier brings Jolivet his horse. He mounts and rides with the Troop that escorts People away.*

## 38. MONTAGE:

*Caravans are formed. Families are loaded onto carts, wagons, the backs of horses, even llamas. The long line of Humanity heads across the vast plain.*

JOLIVET'S NARRATION [*voice-over*]: "It was like a great mass exodus from Biblical times. Where would all these people go? And what would they find when they arrived at unknown destinations?"

## 39. THE HARBOR - EXT/DAY

*People crowd onto the boats in a rush. The 'Caucasus' fills up rapidly as Passengers line the dock.*

## 40. THE 'CAUCASUS' - EXT/DAY

*Smoke from the steamboat billows as it prepares for launch. The First Officer turns People away who haven't paid for space. Merchants argue. One slips the First Officer a bribe so he and his Family can board. More People crowd the dock.*

*Michael shows his pass, his name is checked off. He boards. From the rail he surveys the Crowd. On the bridge, the Captain studies the river's current.*

*Suddenly, Michael sees Nadia down on the dock. She struggles to push through the crowd. She reaches the gangplank of the 'Caucasus', but the First Officer is about to cast off. He won't let her through.*

NADIA: Please! You must let me pass!

FIRST OFFICER: Madam, do you have a ticket?

NADIA: Not yet....

FIRST OFFICER: Are you on the passenger list? No.

NADIA: I have to get on. I can get enough money!

FIRST OFFICER: There will be another boat in three days. I'm sorry.

NADIA: That will be too late! I can pay part of the fare now....

*She pulls out some coins, but the jostling Crowd causes her to drop them, the coins falling into the water.*

NADIA: No!

*The First Officer is amused. He moves closer to Nadia and whispers intimately.*

FIRST OFFICER: Perhaps something can be arranged. You are very beautiful. I'll do you this favor...and you can do me a favor, also.

*Nadia stares angrily at the First Officer's insinuation. She's desperate, but won't take this insult. Suddenly, a hand pats the First Officer's shoulder. He turns, irritated. Michael stands there.*

STROGOFF: Thank you for finding my sister.

FIRST OFFICER: Sister?

STROGOFF: Of course.

*Nadia stares at Michael, then smiles in relief. Michael hands coins to the First Officer.*

NADIA: Why did you leave me at the inn, Brother?

STROGOFF: I thought it best to get to the boat and re-
serve our place. I'm sorry the crowds were so
difficult.

*Michael helps Nadia aboard. The First Officer watches
them strangely.*

## 41. MONTAGE:

*'Caucasus' pulls away from the dock. Smoke rises in the sky,
birds flying in the vapor. Other boats set sail on the sparkling
waters.*

*Landscape passes by as the passengers watch. Novgorod re-
cedes in the distance. A caravan of Exiles moves along the
shore—and Nadia's eyes sadly follow them until the river turns
and they're no longer seen.*

## 42. ON BOARD 'CAUCASUS' - INT/DAY

*Michael and Nadia stand at the railing. They're comfortable
with each other.*

NADIA: I feel so sorry for all those people. What have
they done?

STROGOFF: Perhaps nothing. But the government has to
be careful these days.

NADIA: I appreciate what you did for me, Mr.—?

STROGOFF: Nicholas Korpanoff.

NADIA: I'm Nadia Fedor.

STROGOFF: My pleasure.

NADIA: You have business in Perm, Mr. Korpanoff?

*Michael nods.*

NADIA: I'm on my way to Irkutsk.

*Michael's eyes brighten.*

STROGOFF: That's a very long journey. And difficult.

*Nadia stares out at the water. Now there is only wilderness on the distant shore.*

NADIA: Do you think there is any truth to these rumors of war?

STROGOFF: Yes.

NADIA: It's awful, isn't it.

STROGOFF: Miss Fedor, perhaps you should consider postponing your journey to Irkutsk. If there is danger it'll be the worst on the frontier.

NADIA: It's urgent for me. You see, my father is there. He waits for me.

*Nadia stares at Michael, but he's silent and thoughtful.*

NADIA: Thank you again for your help, sir.

*She walks away, and Michael keeps watching her. He obviously cares. After a moment his eyes drift down to the lower deck, where a load of Peasants and Gypsies create places for themselves to sleep.*
*The deck is crowded. Tents are erected.*
*Sangarre stares from the Crowd, her eyes carefully gliding across the upper deck Passengers, and the ship's Officers. Toma the Bohemian sits near her, wrapped in a blanket. Zurevno is also there, in a large coat and scarf. A grim expression creases his face, his eyes study the river.*

SANGARRE: Victor? Are you sad to be leaving your home?

ZUREVNO: No, Sangarre. I am fine. Very fine.

*The sun beats upon the rippling water like fire.*

☙

## 43. THE TARTAR CAMP - EXT/DAY

*A huge bonfire blazes on a hill above thousands of tents. Feofar Khan and his Chieftains sit in a circle around the flames. Behind them is a map of stretched hide. Murga-Ti paints red flames upon certain territories.*
*Anna, the Girl-Captive, is pushed toward the Men by a Mongol Woman. She carries a tray with bowls and bottles. The Girl seems in a daze of fear, now dressed Tartar fashion*

*in fur and bone. One Chieftain touches her hair affectionately.*

*The Khan sits quietly, eyes closed as if entranced. The Chieftains are careful not to talk so loudly or disturb him.*

*Suddenly, a light tinkling bell is heard, the rhythm of walking. The circle opens for Roola, the Shamaness, who wears the bell on her ankle. Feofar Khan opens his eyes and stares at the Old Woman with affection.*

*He claps his hands loudly. Everyone rises and walks to a nearby tree. A reindeer has been killed, it hangs upside down. Feofar Khan nods to Murga-Ti, who hands Roola an ornate lance. The Old Woman quickly slices the reindeer's belly, intestines roll out. They glisten in the sun.*

*Everyone again sits, this time surrounding the animal. Roola holds the entrails and studies them carefully.*

ROOLA: I see fire. Storms of flame....

*The Chieftains are transfixed by her.*

ROOLA: The fire is everywhere across the earth. A cleansing. The People wish it, they need it to be so. I see many armies. A great battle....

*The Khan nods his head with anticipation.*

ROOLA: The bones of many warriors feed the earth. The tears of many women fill the rivers. I see a great city....

*Murga-Ti stares at the hide map, the symbol of a Fortress.*

ROOLA: Fire surrounds this city. The sky is inflamed, even
        the water. The ice, the snow…it is strange. Flames
        sail down the river like the Devil's boat of death.

*The Khan smiles and whispers to himself.*

FEOFAR KHAN: Irkutsk.

*The Shamaness sifts through more entrails with her bony
fingers.*

ROOLA: There is a very great light. Power lives in this
        light. You, Feofar Khan, live there, also.

*The Khan stares at her with excitement. The Old Woman
reaches deep into the entrails and covers her hands in rich red
blood.*
*She reaches over to him and marks his face with the blood,
his eyes and forehead.*

ROOLA: The people must awaken. You must do it with
        your light, Feofar Khan.

*The Chieftains watch with awe. The Khan's eyes blaze with
dark intensity. His tongue licks a bit of blood at the corner of
his mouth. He reaches into the entrails and covers his hands
red.*

ROOLA: The people must awaken!

*The Khan stands, the Chieftains follow. He walks to the
edge of the hill. Far below are Warriors and People, standing*

*in silence. The Khan towers before them, his eyes mad with lust and power. He raises his blood-covered hands and an immense shout of triumph emerges from the Crowd.*

*Warriors raise their weapons in the air, Mothers raise their Babies high. Then Everyone goes silent as the Khan speaks.*

FEOFAR KHAN: For one hundred moons, the Barbarians have sought to destroy us! They have cast a spell with their iron to keep us from this good land the Gods gave to us! It is now time to break this spell and drown the Barbarians in their own blood!

*He raises his bloody hands again and the People go wild.*

*Warriors mount their horses, and ride off in the direction the Khan indicates. Each Large Group heads toward a different point, and from the high hill they seem to create a living compass.*

*Roola returns to the fire alone. She takes up a cup from the tray and drinks. With hatred she stares at Anna, who watches the spectacle from the edge of the hill.*

*Roola walks over to the Young Girl and viciously shoves her from behind. Anna tumbles down the cliff, her body smashing to a pulp on the rocks far below.*

ر

## 44. THE 'CAUCASUS' - EXT/NIGHT

*A bright moon is reflected on the river as the steamboat makes its way.*

*On deck, the Bohemian purchases bread and rum from another Gypsy, who is talking about something intensely. The*

*Bohemian listens quietly, then takes the food over to Sangarre and Zurevno, who sit in a lean-to facing the water.*
    *Toma sits and passes them the food.*

BOHEMIAN: I have news! Very important, Colonel!

ZUREVNO: Lower your voice.

BOHEMIAN: Yes, sir. But please listen. A courier has been
        sent from the capitol!

ZUREVNO: So?

BOHEMIAN: This courier has possession of a special dis-
        patch that concerns the Colonel directly.

SANGARRE: Who told you?

*Toma points to the Gypsy near the tent, whom Sangarre acknowledges.*

SANGARRE: We must believe this, Victor. Old Louis hears
        many things. And he wears many Russian scars,
        as you do.

ZUREVNO: What is the courier's name?

BOHEMIAN: No one knows. But his message is for the
        Grand Duke in Irkutsk. And it concerns your
        plans.

*Zurevno smiles grimly.*

ZUREVNO: What plans would those be, Toma?

*The Bohemian is silent and tense. Sangarre is irritated.*

SANGARRE: Victor, Toma risked his life to contact Feofar Khan on your behalf.

ZUREVNO: Is this true?

*The Bohemian nods nervously.*

ZUREVNO: And what did the great Khan say?

BOHEMIAN: He awaits your pleasure, sir.

*The Colonel laughs strangely.*

SANGARRE: It is important, Victor, about this courier. He must be stopped.

*The Colonel seems amused, and this bothers the Woman.*

SANGARRE: Why are you not worried?

ZUREVNO: Because all this courier can say is what everyone will soon know. That I have escaped. That is all. No one can know what is in store for the Grand Duke.

SANGARRE: What do you plan? The fortress at Irkutsk is
impregnable.

ZUREVNO: Sangarre, my love…there is no city on this
earth that cannot be taken.

*The Woman and Bohemian are impressed. They follow*
*Zurevno's eyes to the dining cabin at the upper deck.*

ZUREVNO: Do you see those good Russians up there?
Having their good supper?

BOHEMIAN: Yes.

ZUREVNO: Do you think they could stop us if we wanted
to take this boat from them? They could not! They
are fat and soft, and all they do is dream.

SANGARRE: Dream about what, Victor?

ZUREVNO: Food and God.

*The Woman and Bohemian think about this.*

ZUREVNO: This is why we'll win. Even if the war goes on
for a hundred years, in the end the Russians will
be conquered.

SANGARRE: You, too, are Russian, Victor.

ZUREVNO: True. But I am different. I have very little use
for food…and I have no use for God at all.


## 45. THE DINING CABIN - INT/NIGHT -
## AT THIS SAME TIME

*Michael enters. The room is filled with Diners. He sees Nadia
alone in a corner, reading that same letter. He takes out the
colored scarf, then thinks better of it and returns it to his
pocket. He walks to her table.*

STROGOFF: Sister Nadia.

*She looks up, startled for a moment.*

NADIA: Oh! Hello.

STROGOFF: May I join you?

NADIA: Yes, of course…Brother Nicholas.

*She seems happy to see him.*

STROGOFF: I'm interrupting.

NADIA: No.

*She shoves her letter back into her book. Michael sits.*

NADIA: I've read this letter from Father so many times
I'm surprised the ink hasn't rubbed off.

STROGOFF: Is it good news?

NADIA: No, unfortunately. But I won't burden you with
my problems.

*She remains silent and solemn. Michael tries to cheer her.*

STROGOFF: Perhaps if we are to be family, we should at
least have supper together.

NADIA: All right.

*She smiles. Michael signals the porter. Food is immediately delivered on a tray. A standard stew, bread, a bottle of wine.*
*Michael pours two glasses.*

STROGOFF: This wine is French. Have you been to
France, Nadia?

NADIA: I've never left Russia, I'm afraid.

STROGOFF: Well, neither have I.

NADIA: I would like to see Rome. Especially the ancient
temples. Father traveled all over Europe when he
was young. He's a physician. He believes that the
more he learns about the medical practices of
other societies, the better his skills as a healer.

STROGOFF: He's in Irkutsk now?

NADIA: Yes. His life has been unhappy lately.

*They eat, and Michael watches her trustingly.*

STROGOFF: My father is no longer alive. But my mother is.

NADIA: Mother passed away last year. So we really are brother and sister, Nicholas! With my father and your mother still with us!

*They smile at each other and drink more wine. The food is consumed with gusto.*

NADIA: Do you think that if a man has been exiled, it is possible for him to be pardoned someday?

STROGOFF: Maybe.

*She leans across to him and whispers.*

NADIA: Can you keep a secret, Nicholas? What I tell you must never be mentioned to anyone.

*Michael nods, humoring her.*

NADIA: My father is Wassili Fedor.

*She expects recognition, but Michael just looks at her.*

NADIA: Wassili Fedor! The private physician to all the
Moscow aristocrats…and even sometimes to the
Czar himself!

STROGOFF: I see.

NADIA: He was sent away to Irkutsk. The reasons were
absurd…but people are so afraid of what they
don't understand.

STROGOFF: He was ordered out of the territory?

NADIA: The soldiers tore him from my mother's arms
and led him to the frontier! Months later Mother
died of a broken heart!

STROGOFF: I'm very sorry.

NADIA: Have you ever heard of the Society of Illuminati?

STROGOFF: Isn't it a secret group of magicians or alche-
mists?

NADIA: Seekers! That is all! Seekers after the Truth of the
Great Mysteries. My father was a member of this
private society. They have meetings where they
exchange information, scientific knowledge that
can help people, philosophical ideas. Several of
Father's patients discovered that he was an
Illuminatus. This is the stupid reason he was sent
into exile!

*Michael pours them more wine. He's fascinated. Nadia is filled with intense passion.*

NADIA: For awhile I despised the Czar and all his court for what they did. After Mother died, I was so bitter and filled with rage! I would have burnt down the Kremlin if given the chance! But now I just want to join Father and see him happy in his last days.

STROGOFF: You no longer feel any hate?

NADIA: People are simple. They believe what they want to. Yet I trust that there is goodness in everyone… and perhaps someday my father will be vindicated.

STROGOFF: He's fortunate to have someone who loves him so much.

*They stare at each other, a bit embarrassed. Then their eyes shift to the bright moon reflected outside on the water.*

## 46. SLEEPING QUARTERS - INT/NIGHT - LATER

*They walk down the corridor between berths. They're both a bit tipsy from the wine. Nadia puts her arm in Michael's, he steadies her. Both of them are unsure about these new feelings. They reach Michael's cabin. Nadia pulls away from him.*

NADIA: I should go back on deck and sleep there.

STROGOFF: Please. You take the cabin.

NADIA: I don't want to drive you from your bed, Nicholas.

*Michael opens the door for her.*

STROGOFF: I'll be fine. I'm not even tired.

NADIA: It isn't fair to you.

*She looks at him fondly. He goes into the cabin, lights a lamp, then pulls a blanket from the bed and steps back out the door. Nadia grabs his arm, stares into his eyes, then kisses his lips lightly.*

NADIA: Thank you.

*She goes into the cabin and closes the door. Michael touches his lips, then removes the colored scarf from his coat and hangs it over the door-knob. He walks away smiling.*

## 47. THE UPPER DECK - EXT/NIGHT

*Michael settles into a deck chair, the blanket wrapped tightly around him. He watches the stars above, but his eyes slowly close from weariness.*

*The night is quiet and peaceful. Calm waves rock the boat as it makes its way along the river.*

*Dark clouds cover the face of the moon.*

*Now Michael is almost asleep, but not fully. Whispering voices from below cause him to come alert.*

BOHEMIAN'S VOICE: He does not seem concerned about this dangerous courier. Why is this?

SANGARRE'S VOICE: He doesn't always say what he is thinking.

*Michael slowly rises from the chair and peers to the lower deck, trying to see who speaks. But all is darkness there.*

BOHEMIAN'S VOICE: The courier must be found, and stopped!

SANGARRE'S VOICE: I agree. We do not need this trouble.

*All is silent. Michael holds his breath with tension. He only sees many tents and yurts down below, and all he hears is occasional snoring.*

*Michael quietly slides his deck chair into a corner, where he is hidden by shadows. He takes out his long knife and holds it under the blanket.*

*His face is grim, his eyes wide. Sleep only comes to him in brief episodes as he stays prepared.*

৩

## 48. THE CZAR'S CHAMBER - INT/DAY

*A brown cat climbs the silk curtain above the nightingale's cage. The bird flutters in fear as the cat stalks it. Its claws reach into the cage—*

PRINCESS LARA: Mephisto! You stop that!

*As the Little Girl screams, the cat leaps from the curtain and hides under a table. The Princess catches it by the tail.*

PRINCESS LARA: You're a very bad kitty, Mephisto. You leave Goldy alone.

*The cat purrs in her arms.*

PRINCESS LARA: If you weren't so pretty I'd spank you.

*Lara hears footsteps outside, Men's voices. She quickly ducks under a table to hide. The cat meows, but the Princess holds it tightly so it'll stay quiet.*
*Czar Alexander, General Nerensky, and Major Torlov enter. They've been involved in intense discussions. Princess Lara scoots deeper under the table to watch and listen secretly.*

NERENSKY: If we had more spies on the frontier things would be less confusing. I implore you, Sire. In the future we must have more thorough means of gathering intelligence.

CZAR ALEXANDER: Yes.

TORLOV: I would like to add one point, if I may.

NERENSKY: Say your mind, Major.

TORLOV: Our intelligence sources must come from the army. They must be trained to know what to look for and how to report back competently. There is nothing more maddening than to receive word from a potato farmer or a milk maid that they saw some Tartars in the hills…but they can't remember how many. Or if they were equipped for battle or simply a hunting party looking to steal livestock.

NERENSKY: False reports, inadequate information… sometimes it's worse than no information at all. We cannot mobilize based on illusion, especially since the frontier is such a long distance from our main forces.

*The Czar listens intently.*

CZAR ALEXANDER: What about these couriers we use?

NERENSKY: The couriers are excellent intelligence officers. The only drawback is that many of their missions last for only a brief period of time. The men are not in the field long enough to establish themselves at a particular site where they could gather more thorough information.

TORLOV: The couriers ride in, deliver a message, obtain a
        reply, then ride out again. But what they witness
        is usually extraordinary, because many times
        they're the first to go to the heart of the conflict.

CZAR ALEXANDER: What of this Strogoff? He's a friend
        of yours, is he not, Major?

TORLOV: Yes, Sire.

CZAR ALEXANDER: When do we expect to hear from
        Strogoff?

TORLOV: His orders were to travel directly to Irkutsk. I
        have no doubt that the Lieutenant will come into
        contact with the Tartars. He's a smart man. If they
        don't know who he really is, perhaps he'll be left
        alone. But we may never hear from him until
        Grand Duke Theodore does…because once past
        the Ural Mountains there will be no workable
        telegraph.

CZAR ALEXANDER: Are you sure of this, Major?

TORLOV: Yes, Sire.

NERENSKY: It is our opinion that we must march imme-
        diately. Speed is essential.

*The Czar is thoughtful. Beneath the table, Lara watches
her worried Father. The cat struggles in her arms so she lets it*

*go. Mephisto climbs onto the Czar's desk and walks across his map. Alexander throws the beast off violently.*

CZAR ALEXANDER: Where would Strogoff be at this moment?

NERENSKY: Assuming he has not had difficulties, he should be nearing Perm by steamboat.

CZAR ALEXANDER: Are there hostile forces near that city?

TORLOV: We received a message from Captain Ravski. He has left Perm and is scouting the territory west of the Urals. He reports that the populace is filled with unrest and fear, but that no Tartars have been spotted in the area.

NERENSKY: That journalist is with Ravski. The Frenchman.

TORLOV: He's a fine fellow, Jolivet. I'm sure he'll have commendable things to say to his countrymen about your Empire, Sire.

*The Czar studies his map solemnly.*

CZAR ALEXANDER: What I am concerned about is the safety of my people. That is the most important thing to me.

*He looks sadly at the Two Soldiers.*

CZAR ALEXANDER: I want them stamped out! Annihilated! Every Tartar we find must be destroyed! Women and children as well!

*Princess Lara stares in fear at her angry Father, her eyes wide and confused.*

CZAR ALEXANDER: We must wipe them from the face of the earth! Or they will keep breeding like lice…and always be a threat to us!

*The Soldiers nod in agreement.*

∽

## 49. A FOREST VALLEY - EXT/DAY

*The Russian Troops ride along a narrow trail under towering trees. Jolivet watches Captain Ravski talk enthusiastically to his men. In the far distance, many miles away, are jagged snow-capped peaks.*

JOLIVET'S NARRATION [*voice-over*]: "The Ural Mountains seemed like silver towers belonging to a kingdom of giants. Captain Ravski insisted our party would reach them in two days, then the scouting mission would be complete. As we rode along this peaceful trail, I expected only glory. But the Fates are known to have great fun with fools…."

An arrow suddenly slices through the neck of a Young Soldier. Another Man is shot in the back. They fall from their horses, and the Troops stare at the bodies. Then a wave of arrows fill the sky, Jolivet taking one in the leg.

Ravski draws his sword. Suddenly the Tartars ride wildly down upon them from both sides of the valley. They yell savagely, firing their guns and cross-bows. More surprised Russians fall bleeding to the ground.

Ravski orders his Troop to head for a grove of trees, but before he can rally them a bullet finds his heart. Jolivet sees the Captain fall, and for a moment forgets about his own pain. Then he spurs his horse to follow the covered supply wagon, but Warriors topple it with logs pulled behind their horses. The Driver is shot. Jolivet's horse bucks in fear as the wagon falls, and the Journalist is thrown. The horse falls on top of the wagon.

The Russians are seriously outnumbered. It's a massacre, the new Troops no match for the renegade Tartars. Many Young Soldiers try running for cover but are cut down with lances. Some are run to the ground, their heads split by axes.

The Soldiers who stand and fight cannot hold against the onslaught. The Tartar horses leap over bushes into the line of Troops. Another wave of arrows coming from the hillside find their marks. Bullets kill animals as well as Men.

Very few Tartars are killed, and many of these are the Warriors who leave their mounts to run crazily at the Russians with knives or lances. Sometimes it takes several Soldiers to bring one Man down. This distraction allows other Tartars time to invade the line of Riflemen.

Chaos! Dust and blood! Screams of pain and fear amidst the trees!

## 50. THE BATTLEFIELD - EXT/DAY - AFTERWARD

*The ground is soaked in blood. Flies swarm on the Corpses. At the overturned wagon, a hand squirms in the dirt and Jolivet crawls out. There's a gash on his head, and his leg is bleeding.*

*Like a madman he wanders amongst the Dead. Bodies hang burnt from trees. Eyes have been removed, sex organs, limbs. Severed heads are stuck atop lances.*

*Captain Ravski has been hanged, his body shot with twenty or thirty arrows.*

JOLIVET'S NARRATION [*voice-over*]: "How can men be so cruel to other men? Is nothing sacred, not even honorable death? I wanted to curse God for creating us if this Hell-on-earth was to be the final result of civilized efforts. It was a miracle that I had survived, but why hadn't the gift extended to some of these young soldiers?"

*Jolivet slumps to the ground and weeps.*

*After a moment, he hears a distinct whinny. In the far trees is a horse, still saddled. There's blood on its flank, but the animal seems strong. Jolivet carefully walks to it, trying not to spook him. He grabs the reins and mounts, a painful effort with his wounded leg. He rides away as fast as he can.*

∽

# 51. THE 'CAUCASUS', ON DECK - EXT/DAY

*Michael stares at the crowd of Peasants and Gypsies on the lower deck, searching all the faces. Tents come down, Yurts are packed up.*

*Nadia approaches, so he's now distracted. She wears the scarf.*

NADIA: It's beautiful. Thank you, Nicholas.

STROGOFF: Did you sleep well?

NADIA: Yes. Are we near Perm?

*As he is answering her question, the steamboat whistle blows. The 'Caucasus' rounds a bend in the river...and the quay is filled with People, a frightening number of Exiles and Refugees. They yell at the boat, desperate to get on board.*

*On the bridge, the Captain and First Officer study the spectacle.*

FIRST OFFICER: What does this mean?

CAPTAIN: I don't know. But they'll tear the boat apart!

*The Captain turns the wheel, steering the 'Caucasus' onto a new course.*

FIRST OFFICER: Where are we headed?

CAPTAIN: There's a quiet harbor farther south. Other vessels are behind us. Let them deal with this mob!

*On the lower deck, Zurevno, Sangarre, and the Bohemian watch the angry Mass of People. Some Refugees dive into the river and swim frantically for the boat, but it's futile. Old Louis joins them at the rail.*

OLD LOUIS: If you want my opinion, the Czar is ruining this country. Many of those people have been run out of their own homes!

*Zurevno is solemn.*

ZUREVNO: There is always a reason for revolution. It's never something simply born from thin air.

## 52. ON THE RIVER, BEYOND PERM - EXT/DAY LATER

*The 'Caucasus' pulls into the small harbor, containing only a few small junks.*

*Michael again studies the Crowd, but the faces are unfamiliar. His eyes drift across Zurevno in his cloak, the Bohemian, Old Louis, Sangarre…who stares up at him, then looks away quickly.*

*Nadia sets her small bag at his feet.*

NADIA: I thought we'd be landing at Perm.

STROGOFF: It's safer here on the outskirts. The Captain
is very smart.

*Nadia is worried.*

NADIA: You'll be going back to the city now, won't you,
Nicholas?

*Michael looks at her sympathetically—and makes his decision.*

STROGOFF: No, Nadia. I've decided my business in Perm
can wait. I'll be going on to Irkutsk.

NADIA: I see.

STROGOFF: If you'd allow me to continue traveling with
you, perhaps as brother and sister we can expedite this journey…share expenses…make it more
efficient for us both?

*She gazes at him with gratitude.*

NADIA: It would be my pleasure, Mr. Korpanoff.

*He lifts her small bag. They look out across the near-empty
dock…to stables and a stock-yard.*
*They disembark.*

NADIA: Is this a place to find adequate transportation?

*Michael smiles and stares at horses in a corral.*

∽

## 53. A FOREST - EXT/DAY

*Riding in an open coach, the wind blows Michael's and Nadia's hair. The bearded Driver wildly cracks his whip above four fine horses' heads. The trees seem to rush by as the coach speeds down the trail. Mountains loom in the distance.*

*They drink vodka. Michael offers the bottle to Nadia, who sips. He knocks on the Driver's shoulder, and he takes the bottle. Michael also passes him some bread.*

DRIVER: Should we stop and rest, sir?

STROGOFF: No.

DRIVER: Good. I admire people who know where they're going and don't waste time.

STROGOFF: How long before the next post-station?

DRIVER: Perhaps two or three hours. It's near the foot-hills where the mountains begin to rise.

STROGOFF: Can you get us there before nightfall?

DRIVER: Yes.

*Nadia leans back and watches a hawk gliding across a cloud. Light snow flurries filter down into her hair, and she wraps her coat tightly.*

*The horses gallop with abandon.*

## 54. A CREEK - EXT/DAY - LATER

*They've stopped the coach briefly on the bank. Horses graze in the grass. In the bushes, the Driver relieves himself.*
   *Nadia combs her hair, straightening out the tangles from the wind. Michael splashes cold water in his face at the creek.*
   *The Driver buttons the front of his pants and walks over to them.*

DRIVER: Sorry about the delay, Mr. Korpanoff.

STROGOFF: It's all right. No harm in taking a rest.

DRIVER: The horses will be better for it, that's certain.

   *He stares at Nadia, her beauty compelling.*

DRIVER: I hope the ride isn't too rough for you and your
      brother, miss.

NADIA: It's not. What was your name again?

DRIVER: Lorgi, miss.

NADIA: Well, you're a fine driver, Mr. Lorgi.

   *He's happy hearing this, yet notices Michael's tooth neck-lace.*

DRIVER: What poor hunter did you buy that from?

STROGOFF: I actually…was given it by a good friend.

DRIVER: Is he still alive, this friend?

STROGOFF: We're very close.

*Nadia looks at the necklace strangely. It's her first time seeing it. Michael quickly covers it with the shirt.*

DRIVER: If God was a bear we'd all be devils! You can't trust them. One day my wife brought home a bear-skin rug. She bought it from a Turk, who told her he'd got it from a Chinaman. If it was such good quality, why'd everybody sell it off, I ask her. But she says we should just be grateful for God's gifts and not question a fine bargain. But I'm a superstitious man. One night I hear a sound. I light a candle, walk down the stairs. Nothing's there. But something bites my foot. I bleed. I fire my rifle in the dark, this wakes my wife. She lights a lamp and calls me a fool. Do you know what I think took a hunk out of my foot? That bear-skin rug. There was blood on the teeth. So even when they're dead, those beasts are dangerous!

*Nadia and Michael laugh.*

## 55. ACROSS A PLAIN - EXT/DAY - LATER

*As the coach passes, quail are flushed from bushes. Snow flurries are more apparent. Dark clouds collect in the sky, blotting out the sun.*

*The coach seems tiny in the wide expanse, and the Ural Mountains loom nearby.*

*Dusk begins to fade across the grasses. Inside the coach, Nadia sleeps, her head resting on Michael's shoulder. He watches her timidly and brushes hair from her face. He watches the clouds collect in the sky, the darkness over the mountains.*

*In the distance is the post-station. The coach speeds toward it.*

*The Driver reins in the horses. Billowing dust enshrouds them as they stop in front of the small building and corral.*

*Michael taps Nadia's shoulder, her sleepy eyes open.*

STROGOFF: We're here.

*The Woman rubs her eyes, then stares in awe at the mountains that tower above her. Thunder rumbles in the high peaks.*

*An Old Caretaker waves at them in welcome from the porch.*

## 56. THE POST-STATION - INT/DUSK

*They are seated at a long wooden table, except Michael, who stares at the window toward the high mountains. The Old Caretaker brings a kettle of soup for the Driver and Nadia.*

STROGOFF: Can you drive at night, Lorgi?

DRIVER: Certainly. If the price is fair.

*Michael lays some money on the table by the man's spoon.*

STROGOFF: We must keep going.

CARETAKER: A storm is coming. You should stay the
    night, at least.

STROGOFF: No. We've lost enough time. Am I correct,
    sister?

NADIA: Yes.

CARETAKER: You're crazy, but you're not alone. Some-
    one else came through a couple of hours ago. He
    wouldn't stay, either.

*Michael breaks off a chunk of bread.*

STROGOFF: Who was this man?

CARETAKER: I don't know his name. But he was in some
    sort of trouble. There was blood on him.

STROGOFF: He didn't say what happened?

CARETAKER: It was strange, he didn't speak at all. I felt
    like I was staring at a ghost. He threw some money

at me and pointed to another horse. His was almost ridden to death. It had blood on it, also. I saddled him a new one, invited him in for food. But he shook his head as if the devil had eaten off his tongue. Then he rode off into the mountains like a man possessed!

DRIVER: Very odd.

*The Old Caretaker wipes soup from his beard.*

CARETAKER: This is a time when we'll see many strange things on the road. You mark my words.

NADIA: Why do you say this?

CARETAKER: The world is not what it seems, Miss. That's all I mean.

*Nadia nods, solemnly understanding.*

STROGOFF: Have there been any sightings of…hostile forces?

CARETAKER: You mean the Tartars? No. But I should tell you, there are many caves up there. And more trails than veins in a man's hand.

STROGOFF: This is not the only pass?

CARETAKER: No, young man. Certainly not. This range

of peaks spreads for a great many miles. But this is one of the most well-traveled roads, and one of the easiest for a coach or wagon.

*Michael stares again at the pass as red dusk-light enchants it.*

STROGOFF: Do you think there are many routes that most people wouldn't know about?

CARETAKER: That's what I said! Why are you asking so many questions, young fellow? Are you a spy for the Khan?

*Michael smiles ironically, and the Driver laughs.*

DRIVER: No, old man. Mr. Korpanoff and his sister are actually the Czar and Czarina! On holiday! It's a secret, so you mustn't tell anyone, or we'll be followed forever and mobbed by all their loyal subjects who dream about touching their royal garments or bathing in their divine breath!

*Everyone laughs with delight at the sarcasm, but Michael's amusement is definitely an act.*

## 57. THE STATION YARD - EXT/DUSK - LATER

*Lorgi harnesses new horses to the coach. Nadia climbs up, settles in under blankets and furs. Then she looks toward the station window at Michael, still inside. He's expertly check-*

*ing over one of the Old Caretaker's rifles. Nadia sees him give the old man some money, wrap the weapon in a blanket, then carry it out to the coach nonchalantly.*

*She questions him with her eyes, but he stashes the rifle under the seat without comment.*

*The Driver lights the hanging lamps.*

DRIVER: I must tell you, Mr. Korpanoff…this rain that's coming does not look good!

STROGOFF: You've driven in storms before, haven't you?

DRIVER: Yes, but I am nervous about this one. And my horses are nervous also.

*Michael takes some more money from his purse and sticks it in the Driver's coat pocket.*

STROGOFF: Do you feel calmer now, Mr. Lorgi?

DRIVER: Yes, sir. Quite calm for the moment.

*They mount the coach. The Driver cracks his whip and they head toward the pass. The Old Caretaker watches the distant dangling lamps until the dark peaks seem to swallow the coach whole.*

∾

## 58. THE MOUNTAIN PASS - EXT/NIGHT

*The night seems ready to bust open on the slope. Distant thunder mumbles. They ride in silence.*

The rain begins. At first it's mild, then lightening cracks, flashing brightly across the rocks. The rain pours down.

The coach manages as the horses keep moving, climbing in the rocks. But the Driver has fear in his eyes.

More lightning fills the sky. The towering peaks are awesome.

The ground becomes muddy in the downpour. The horses have a more difficult time, since the slope is steep.

The Driver stops the coach, then climbs down to lead the team by harness. Nadia is worried. Michael is also concerned, but they push on.

Gradually, the trail is thick with mud. Puddles form. The lead horse slips and falls, nearly spooking the others, but the Driver steadies them expertly. Michael jumps from the coach to help. He and Lorgi control the team, and Nadia also jumps down to lighten the coach.

They move high into the mountains.

Harsh wind rolls through the pass, blasting them. The rain is a slashing torrent. The lamps go out, so now it's dark except for sporadic lightning flashes.

Broken tree limbs are hurled across the trail by the wind. They catch on the wheels of the coach. Nadia pulls one out. Suddenly a tall tree breaks and crashes so close to the road they have to try to clear it. Nadia holds the team while Michael's horses are spooked. They begin to walk backward, Nadia can't control them alone. Michael runs to help. The tired and frightened animals refuse to go forward. Lorgi strikes them again and again with his whip, then they finally obey.

The trail is rough. A back wheel sinks into a pothole of mud and water, stopping the coach. Michael goes to the rear and pushes, lifting with all his might until his teeth grind *with the effort. Lorgi screams at the horses, and the coach finally jolts loose.*

*Up ahead is the peak. They reach it and almost fall with exhaustion. The mountain has leveled. out. The Driver laughs hysterically and collapses against a rock wall. Lightning flashes to reveal a sheltered outcropping and a shallow cave.*

## 59. IN THE CAVE - EXT/NIGHT - LATER

*The coach is in place, shielding the opening. The horses lay at rest under a ledge. A fire blazes in the cave. Nadia, Michael, and Lorgi are drenched and shivering before the flames. Thunder and lightning still roar around them, but a tarp keeps the rain from coming in.*

*A bottle of brandy is passed around.*

DRIVER: We can descend at daylight. It would be suicide to try in the dark.

NADIA: I agree.

STROGOFF: We have no other choice, it seems. No matter what my duty demands!

NADIA: Duty?

*She stares at him, and Michael realizes he's said too much. He stares into the fire so she won't ask again.*

*They close their eyes to try to rest. Suddenly, Michael thinks he hears something: the distant whinny of a horse! He sits up, hears it again: a horse's tormented cry of pain. Lorgi has heard it also.*

*The Driver pokes his head back out through the tarp. All four horses seem fine. But again, the distant sound of that awful whinny.*

STROGOFF: What is that? Are there wild horses in these mountains?

*The Driver shakes his head fearfully.*

DRIVER: It could be anything…or anyone! Even a demon!

*More lightning and thunder crashes so loudly that Nadia also sits up and wonders. The disturbing animal's cry continues.*

STROGOFF: I'm going to see.

*He lifts the rifle from the coach, but then changes his mind about taking it. He hands the weapon to Nadia instead.*

STROGOFF: Have you used one of these, sister?

NADIA: Don't you remember? I used to hunt with our father many times.

*Michael nods appreciatively then goes out again into the storm. Nadia watches him move down the trail and out of sight.*

DRIVER: Miss, forgive me for saying this. Your brother is
very brave, but he's also very foolish.

*Nadia glares at the Man although she worries that he's
right.*


## 60. ON A RIDGE - EXT/NIGHT

*As Michael stalks, the anguished sound becomes louder. Trees
sway, creating ominous shadows. More branches are slung
across the rocks and onto the trail. He takes out his pistol and
large hunting knife, holding the weapons ready.*

*Suddenly, lightning strikes a tree. It's immediately engulfed
in flame. Michael watches it in awe and fear, then walks
carefully past.*

*At a bend in the trail, the horse cry is very distinct, but
Michael still can't see anything. The cry is eery and ghost-like
in the darkness and rain...but some of the light from the
burning tree allows him to discover a ledge.*

*He looks down. A horse lies smashed on some rocks below,
its large neck bone protruding through the hide. But to
Michael, the strangest sight is the Man!*

*Jolivet sits on a boulder staring off the mountainside into
space. His back is to Michael, who has to yell to get the
Journalist's attention.*

STROGOFF: Are you hurt?

*Jolivet slowly turns around, and Michael is shocked to see
the Man's torn, bloody face. Michael recognizes him, but Jolivet
seems dazed.*

JOLIVET: Are you speaking to me?

STROGOFF: I believe you're the only fellow down there.

*Jolivet stares through the rain, then smiles strangely.*

JOLIVET: I know you. You're the sweet Angel of Death.

*Michael can't help but smile at the Journalist's strange morbidity.*

STROGOFF: Do you want me to pull you up? Or would you rather spread your wings and fly off the edge?

JOLIVET: For the last several hours I've thought about doing little else.

STROGOFF: Untie the halter and reins from the horse. Then tie a small stone to the end and throw it up to me.

*Jolivet slowly climbs off the rock. He's limping. He gently cradles the horse's broken neck and whispers to it as he slips off the halter.*

JOLIVET: I've caused your ruin…you poor pitiful thing.

*He ties the reins together, then attaches a stone. At the first try throwing it, he can't reach Michael. He tries again, Michael reaches out further and catches it. The Journalist holds tight while Michael hauls him up the cliff.*

*Jolivet collapses in the mud. Now he has a better look at Michael.*

JOLIVET: I do know you.

*Michael is silent about this. He looks down at the suffering horse and he's filled with sympathy. With his pistol he takes careful aim...then fires! The horse no longer suffers.*

*The mountain thunders with the echo. In the distance they hear a rumbling, and they see a mountain of snow fall in the small avalanche created by the noise.*

STROGOFF: I shouldn't have done that.

JOLIVET: No, you did what was kind and merciful.

STROGOFF: Can you walk? Our camp is not far.

*Jolivet nods, Michael helps him up. They move back up the slope, Jolivet limping.*

JOLIVET'S NARRATION [*voice-over*]: "I had been saved again from the dark jaws of death! If I had believed in God anymore I would have thanked him. As it was, I owed my life to this quiet young man. He had appeared out of the night like a mountain spirit to rescue me from Oblivion!"

*The wind is harsh against Jolivet's face. Suddenly the rain transforms into snow, and flakes fall on them heavily.*
*They pass by the burning tree. Jolivet is fascinated by the*

*sight. Michael watches him, noticing the arrow wound to his leg.*

*Jolivet stares at Michael, his glazed eyes reflecting the burning tree.*

JOLIVET: The invasion has begun. All around us there is
         blood…murder!

STROGOFF: Weren't you riding with Captain Ravski's
          troops?

JOLIVET: Yes. Poor man …

STROGOFF: Has something happened to him?

*Jolivet nods his head sadly. Before Michael can ask more, they hear a rifle shot, and screams that are obviously from Nadia!*

*Michael runs as fast as he can, leaving Jolivet behind.*

*There's another scream from Nadia, then a loud growling that's familiar to Michael! He struggles to the top of the slope, straining every muscle to get there quickly!*

## 61. THE CAVE - EXT/NIGHT

*As the ridge levels out, three of the horses gallop wildly by, almost trampling Michael. He must flatten his body against the rock wall. The fourth horse struggles to escape from the claws of a huge brown bear. Nadia is up on a ledge with the rifle. The Driver slaps at the bear with his whip, trying to* chase it away from the horse. The beast bites into the horse's leg, snapping the bone.

It slaps its huge paw at Lorgi, knocking him to the ground.

Nadia sees Michael, yet so does the bear. He growls like a demon and bites another chunk from the horse. Michael nods for Nadia to aim her rifle, and he also aims his pistol. The bear stands on its hind legs and moves toward Michael. The man holds his ground...so does Nadia from the side...and they fire almost simultaneously!

Both bullets hit their mark. The bear falls to the ground, stumbling on all fours. Michael quickly runs toward the wounded animal, his huge knife clutched in his hand—

Nadia watches in astonishment and terror—

Michael jumps on the back of the bear! The wounded animal growls with pain and tries to slap the man off. Michael grips its ear and plunges the knife into the side of its neck. Blood gushes. The bear howls, falls again, rolls—propelling Michael away. It crawls across the rocks trailing blood. Everyone looks on in horror and fascination as it tries to scramble up a cliff, but it has no more strength. The rocks are awash with the bear's blood. It finally crumbles to the mud and breathes its last.

Nadia is pale with fear, yet her eyes are wide with excitement and a strange passion. She stares at Michael, and it's obvious the wild feeling is shared by him.


## 62. AFTERWARD

The remaining horses have been caught. The Men take large tree limbs and trunks, level them under the bear carcass, then *roll it off the cliff. They dispose of the dead horse in the same way.*

## 63. IN THE CAVE - INT/NIGHT - LATER

*Everyone lays by the campfire, tired, ragged, wet and battered. Nadia finishes bandaging Lorgi's arm. Michael hands him the brandy, then it passes to Jolivet, who is telling his story with a quiet, captivating intensity.*

JOLIVET: They came out of nowhere...savages, wild Tartar savages...we were completely outnumbered... even Ravski was caught by surprise. Poor fellow. I've never in all my days seen such butchery...such demonic horror!

## 64. DOWN THE MOUNTAIN - EXT/DAY

*Nadia and the wounded Driver ride in the coach. Jolivet and Michael lead the horses down the steep trail through snow patches.*

STROGOFF: Monsieur, may I ask a question about this battle? I know nothing of military matters...but I was wondering why the Tartars were not first spotted by Captain Ravski's forward scouts?

JOLIVET: There were no scouts.

STROGOFF: Excuse me?

JOLIVET: No scouts. No warning. We rode straight into an ambush.

*Michael is irritated by this news. He grits his teeth, whispering angrily to himself.*
*The Journalist watches him curiously, his recognition of Michael growing.*

JOLIVET: Monsieur Korpanoff, have you spent any time at the Czar's court in Moscow?

STROGOFF: No, I haven't. Why do you ask?

JOLIVET: You remind me of someone. Have you ever served in the Imperial Guard?

STROGOFF: No. I'm merely a simple merchant.

JOLIVET: Sir, you do not handle weapons like a simple merchant. Horses, either.

STROGOFF: Horses are my business, Monsieur. Over the years I've learned how to protect my property.

JOLIVET: Do you travel a great deal?

STROGOFF: A bit.

JOLIVET: You seem to know this territory quite well.

*Michael remains silent, but Jolivet is still very curious. They finally reach the bottom of the slope and pat the horses affectionately for their good work. Snow on the rocks has melted.*

*Before them is a huge grassy plain. Jolivet and Michael climb onto the coach. The Driver is now asleep and snoring loudly, but Nadia doesn't mind.*

*The coach continues onto the wide level land, the horses trotting along capably. They leave the mountains behind.*

∽

## 65. THE SIBERIAN PLAIN - EXT/DAY

*The coach seems so tiny in the expanse, the only sign of Humanity for miles around.*

*Michael stops the coach and looks through his spy-glass. There's a post-station in the distance, with four fresh horses in the corral.*

STROGOFF: We are very near.

*Jolivet squints his eyes in another direction. He sees a trail of moving dust.*

JOLIVET: What is that?

NADIA: We're not alone, I believe.

*Through the glass: Michael sees it's another coach, also racing toward the post-station.*

STROGOFF: Someone heading the same place we are, but very fast. This worries me....

JOLIVET: Tartars?

STROGOFF: No, it's Russians, I'm sure. But there are only four fresh horses at that post station. And we must have them...not this other coach!

JOLIVET: What can we do?

*In answer, Michael suddenly yells at the team and cracks the whip over their heads. The coach lurches forward and races across the plain. The Driver immediately awakens, Nadia is startled. Michael's face is grim with determination.*

*The coach speeds along the grass, veering to miss stones and tree stumps. The horses strain at the bit as Michael wildly urges them on faster—faster—*

*The huge gap between the two coaches narrows, but the distant coach has sped up. It has a full team of four horses, and it's larger. Michael sees Faces looking out, and uniforms. But he's too far away to recognize anyone distinctly.*

*Michael's horses begin to lather, the bits forcing their mouths to bleed. This race is pushing them to the limit. Nadia is excited. Lorgi stares down at the wheels with worry. Michael cracks the whip madly and yells at the team with abandon.*

*Up ahead, the two narrow trails converge into one road. The coaches race to the fork, and it seems like they'll soon collide.*

*Michael's coach beats the other by yards. He crosses its path, veers in front—and Zurevno yells at him from the rival coach.*

*Michael keeps on, the thrill forcing him to laugh. Zurevno, now in uniform, keeps yelling.*

ZUREVNO: Stop! I command you to stop!

*The Bohemian, also in uniform, drives wildly. Two Younger "Soldiers" ride beside him. One of them aims his rifle at Michael, but Zurevno holds his arm.*

ZUREVNO: No, Peter. There are other ways.

*Old Louis and Sangarre are with Zurevno in the coach, also masquerading in Russian Army uniforms. Sangarre stares hatefully as Michael drives away, and her eyes meet Nadia's.*

## 66. THE POST-STATION - EXT/DAY

*Michael's coach pulls up abruptly. Dust fills the yard. The Postmaster comes out with his Wife. The Woman looks at the Driver being helped from the coach by Nadia.*

WIFE: Lorgi! What happened to you?

DRIVER: A bear tried to eat me, but as you see I didn't
          taste very good.

*Michael walks to the corral. The four horses prance around proudly.*

STROGOFF: We need horses badly. These four will do.
       Quickly, please!

*The Postmaster rushes to the coach and starts to unharness
the haggard team. Everyone turns to watch the other coach
race into the station. The "Soldiers" dismount, but their rifles
are held in a hostile way. Zurevno climbs out and stares at
Michael grimly, then orders the Postmaster in his rough voice.*

ZUREVNO: Horses! Now!

*The Postmaster has unhitched Michael's and is leading
them to the corral, but he stops abruptly.*

POSTMASTER: Forgive me, sir. I'm very sorry. There are
       no more horses.

ZUREVNO: What?

POSTMASTER: These four are the last we have. But you
       are welcomed to stay the night. New animals are
       expected tomorrow.

ZUREVNO: I can't wait.

*Michael stares at this Group, yet something about them
seems strange to him. Especially Sangarre in her uniform,
and Old Louis. But he shrugs and turns back to the corral.*

ZUREVNO: What about those?

*He points to the corral, where Michael has gone.*

POSTMASTER: They belong to these travelers. They arrived just before you. The first choice is theirs. That's our policy.

*Zurevno stares at Michael's back, then yells at him.*

ZUREVNO: You! Mister!

*Everyone feels the tension, and is shocked. Michael solemnly turns from the corral.*

ZUREVNO: Government business, mister. You must forfeit this team to us.

STROGOFF: I don't think so.

*Zurevno's eyes glare at Michael, who stiffens.*

ZUREVNO: I have no time to lose. You are in no great hurry that I can see. You will be the one to wait!

STROGOFF: No.

*The Bohemian snickers. Nadia stares at him angrily. The Postmaster is unsure what to do. The Two "Soldiers" stand ready. Peter walks slowly toward Michael, but Zurevno waves him back.*

*Michael holds in his anger and confusion. Zurevno smiles sarcastically, his eyes glistening with challenge.*

ZUREVNO: You refuse to give us your horses? You refuse
to assist the Czar's emissaries?

*Michael grits his teeth, yet stands firm.*

STROGOFF: I, too, have business that cannot wait, sir.

*Zurevno slowly walks toward him, staring at Michael with
curiosity. He suddenly slaps him in the face with his glove!
Michael is enraged, his eyes blaze. His hand immediately goes
to the hilt of his knife…but then he struggles for control.*
*Zurevno steps back and draws his sword.*

ZUREVNO: Defend yourself, mister!

STROGOFF: I will not fight you.

*Peter laughs. The Bohemian throws his sword through the
air and it lands at Michael's feet.*

ZUREVNO: Pick it up.

*Michael quickly takes a step forward, wanting with every
muscle to grab that weapon. He's forced to restrain himself.
His face fills with sweat, he shivers with humiliation. Everyone is shocked by his lack of action. Nadia is confused.*

ZUREVNO: Sir, you are a coward.

*Michael suddenly turns and walks quickly away. His face
twists with self-disgust, but nobody sees his pain as he makes
his way into a grove of trees.*

*Jolivet watches Michael disappear.*

JOLIVET'S NARRATION [*voice-over*]: "How could this
be? How could such a brave young man as this
allow himself to be humiliated and insulted in
such a way? I didn't understand it. Was it because
they were soldiers? Or had he taken ill? No, there
had to be another reason. But it was very strange
and very sad to see."

*Nadia follows Michael. The Soldiers and Bohemian laugh
amongst themselves.*

ZUREVNO: My horses. Quickly!

POSTMASTER: Yes, sir! Right away!

*The Postmaster hurries to unharness Zurevno's horses. Lorgi
limps into the station, disgusted by it all. Jolivet approaches
Zurevno.*

JOLIVET: Monsieur?

ZUREVNO: I am a Colonel.

JOLIVET: Yes, certainly. Colonel, my name is Jolivet. I'm
a journalist.

ZUREVNO: I see. Interesting. You are French?

JOLIVET: Yes.

*Zurevno salutes politely.*

ZUREVNO: I am Colonel Gorlov, Imperial Guard. At your
    service, Monsieur.

JOLIVET: I am honored.

ZUREVNO: And what is a French journalist doing in the
    heart of Russia?

JOLIVET: Well, my story is not a happy one …

*The Two Men walk away chatting like old friends.*


## 67. THE GROVE - EXT/DAY

*Nadia looks for Michael among the trees. She spots him but
remains a discrete distance away. Michael has taken the dispatch pouch from his coat and stares at it in frustration,
mumbling crazily. Nadia cannot hear. He sticks the pouch
back in his coat and there are tears in his eyes.*
    *Nadia steps on dry leaves and startles him.*

NADIA: I don't understand you.

*Michael just shakes his head silently.*
    *They hear a whip crack, the Bohemian's yell, and horses
trotting. They step from the trees and see Zurevno's coach leaving—with Jolivet as one of the passengers.*
    *Nadia reaches for Michael's hand and squeezes it tightly.*

## 68. ZUREVNO'S COACH - INT/DAY

*Old Louis drinks beside the Bohemian and a Soldier. He hands the bottle to Peter inside the coach. Zurevno and Jolivet talk while Sangarre listens carefully.*

JOLIVET: You have a beautiful land, Colonel.

ZUREVNO: As a journalist I'm sure you've seen the entire world.

JOLIVET: Not quite, Monsieur. But Russia is special.

ZUREVNO: Why is this, do you think?

JOLIVET: It is so vast! I have been traveling for many weeks and still I haven't reached a border!

ZUREVNO: You came from Moscow, is that right?

JOLIVET: Yes. I enjoyed the Czar's court very much. His hospitality was superb!

*Zurevno smirks in his sly, secretive way.*

ZUREVNO: Our beloved Alexander is well-renown for his methods of dealing with people.

*Sangarre nods in solemn agreement.*
*Jolivet drinks from the bottle.*

JOLIVET: What is your particular mission at the moment, Colonel Gorlov? If you don't mind my asking?

*Sangarre stares at him suspiciously.*

ZUREVNO: Do I have your word, Monsieur Jolivet, that what I tell you will remain confidential?

JOLIVET: Certainly!

ZUREVNO: It would not do to have Government business read about in the Paris Gazette.

JOLIVET: Colonel Gorlov, you have my word as a gentleman.

*Zurevno takes a sip from the bottle and hands it back to Peter.*

ZUREVNO: We are on the trail of a traitor. My mission is to find this man and exterminate him.

*Jolivet is silent at Zurevno's serious statement. Sangarre stares at the Colonel with disapproval in her eyes.*

ZUREVNO: His name is Victor Zurevno. Have you ever heard of this man?

JOLIVET: I believe so. Is he the one who led the Officer's revolt against the Czar?

*Zurevno nods. Peter smiles subtly, but Sangarre is solemn.*

JOLIVET: Well, Colonel, I'm very impressed! To be entrusted with such a task ...

ZUREVNO: A soldier performs his duty, Monsieur.

*Jolivet takes out his paper and starts to sketch. Zurevno leans over and discovers the picture is of him! He firmly takes the paper from the journalist, rips it into small pieces, then throws it out the coach window.*

ZUREVNO: Secrecy, Monsieur. Discretion!

JOLIVET: Yes! Certainly!

*Sangarre finally smiles.*

## 69. THE POST-HOUSE - INT/DAY - LATER

*Michael and Nadia walk in the door. There is a tense silence as the Postmaster, his Wife, and Lorgi avoid Michael's eyes.*

STROGOFF: My sister and I need horses. When will they arrive?

POSTMASTER: You had them. They were taken from you. Others? Who knows?

STROGOFF: Don't you dare judge me!

POSTMASTER: Any man who allows himself to be spit
        upon and does nothing deserves nothing in re-
        turn.

*In anger Michael suddenly grabs the Postmaster by the coat
and slings him across the room. Lorgi smiles.*

DRIVER: Mr. Korpanoff, leave him. He's a fool. I know
        where there are animals.

## 70. THE HILLS ABOVE THE STATION - EXT/DAY

*Nadia, Michael and Lorgi crouch behind boulders. Below
them is a small valley with a spring and pool of water.*

DRIVER: They will come.

STROGOFF: Are you sure?

DRIVER: Yes. Every afternoon to drink.

*The Men hold long ropes. Suddenly they hear whinnies
and the sound of galloping. Around a bend race five wild
mules. They trot to the water pool like pets.*

DRIVER: I told you.

*He slinks around behind the rocks, as does Michael, until
they're at opposite sides. Then Lorgi whistles shrilly, and he*

*and Michael sling their ropes. Even with a bad arm, Lorgi hits his mark. The mule is captured by the neck.*

*Nadia runs to the bend in the valley. Michael joins her and they wave their arms to steer the mules back. Michael throws his rope and misses. He scrambles onto a rock, throws it again at a different mule, and it slips over the head.*

*The other mules race past Nadia to freedom. She helps Lorgi hold his mule, and Michael has his under control, also.*

DRIVER: They are better than horses! Not as fast, but stronger! Nobody believes me but it's true!

## 71. AFTERWARD

*Michael and Nadia ride away, the mules saddled and equipped. Lorgi waves farewell to them with his good hand.*

☙

## 72. THE PLAINS - EXT/DAY

MONTAGE: *They ride together through the tall grass. It would seem they have no cares. Delight fills their faces, wind blows their hair. Above, a flock of winter swans fly in a wedge. The sun is bright and warms Nadia's and Michael's skin as they travel.*

*They come over a rise and frighten a herd of reindeer. A race begins, the mules running parallel with the deer. Michael and Nadia laugh ecstatically as they run them down. Michael whips out the rifle, sticks the reins in his teeth, and kicks the mule to go faster. He aims and fires. A large reindeer falls! Nadia is in awe of the feat.*

## 73. A GROVE - EXT/NIGHT

*Their campfire glows, its light reflecting off the leaves of trees. A few flutter down to the ground. Reindeer meat roasts over the fire. Michael and Nadia cut chunks from the flank and eat heartily.*

*Sparks from the flames rise in the sky, merging with snow flurries. A few flakes land in Nadia's hair, and she catches others on her tongue.*

*Michael stretches a tarp between the trees to make a tight lean-to. Now they are nearly enclosed. He huddles next to Nadia in the warmth.*

STROGOFF: We made excellent time today. We're very near the river. Tomorrow we can cross over.

*Nadia watches him with contentment.*

NADIA: You're a strange man. You keep secrets.

STROGOFF: There are things…it's better you don't worry about.

NADIA: I want us to trust each other, Nicholas. That officer today, you knew him?

STROGOFF: No.

*Michael shakes his head and Nadia sees he is disturbed. So she changes the subject.*

NADIA: I've never been to Omsk.

STROGOFF: My mother lives there.

NADIA: She does? I didn't know!

STROGOFF: She's an old woman, but still healthy. Marfa
is her name.

NADIA: Then we should see her since we're now brother
and sister.

*She's trying to be amusing, but Michael is obviously wor-
ried.*

STROGOFF: If there has been a conflict in Omsk, I only
hope she was able to get out.

NADIA: We should look for her. Take her with us.

STROGOFF: No.

NADIA: Is she expecting you?

STROGOFF: It wouldn't do.

NADIA: Why, Nicholas? I don't see what reason you would
have to—

*Michael suddenly gets angry.*

STROGOFF: The same reason that makes me stand still while a man slaps me in the face! When I should have cut him down! The same reason that drives me like a madman across this country! Masquerading as a merchant with a sister I don't have!

*Nadia is silent at his outburst.*

STROGOFF: The truth is, there is no reason at all in this world.

*Michael goes quiet, but angrily pokes at the fire with a stick.*

NADIA: Nicholas, I'm not a fool. I'm know you're not entirely what you seem, but I don't care because...I feel affection for you.

STROGOFF: This is dangerous talk.

NADIA: Nicholas, what is troubling you so much?

*He shakes his head in avoidance again, then lays back, his eyes at the sky. Up above in the blue, the stars are bright and clear.*

STROGOFF: Orion.

NADIA: The beautiful brave hunter. With his bow pointed forever in a clear direction across the Universe.

*Nadia touches Michael's hair. She lightly kisses his lips.*

NADIA: You're not alone...unless you want to be.

*He caresses her cheek, then returns the kiss. They both smile into the other's eyes. Nadia hugs Michael exuberantly, then kisses him with even more passion. He winds his fingers into her long hair. Snow flakes again flutter down and catch in the strands, since the lovers have leaned out from under the tarp. Michael wraps a fur tighter around her, and his hand can't resist caressing her breast. Her eyes close, he kisses her neck. He opens her blouse, the skin is so sweet. She kisses his hand, moves as close to him as she can, feels his back moving down on her...his full weight covering her partial nakedness, glowing from the flames. She opens his shirt and kisses his chest, her fingernails running across his skin, making it tingle with heat...and he grips her hard, the passion consuming them...each tasting the other, whispering in pleasure....*

℘

## 74. A FOREST - EXT/DAY

*They ride through the trees without talking. Sunlight streams through the branches onto patches of melting snow.*

*Nadia watches Michael with love in her eyes. He reaches his hand out to her, kisses her fingers.*

*Birds fly from the tops of trees. The wind picks up, rustling the leaves, making more fall. Michael stops his mule and listens carefully.*

NADIA: What?

STROGOFF: It's so quiet …

NADIA: Do you hear? That's the river! We're going the right way, aren't we?

STROGOFF: Yes. But something is strange …

NADIA: You frighten me, Nicholas!

*They stare at each other solemnly.*

STROGOFF: Let's ride!

*They kick their mules and race through the trees at a gallop. Swerving between trunks, ducking limbs, their hair waving in the wind—they ride desperately but with control.*


## 75. THE RIVERBANK - EXT/DAY

*They come out of the trees onto the grass before the Irtych River. They stop their mules and take a breath from the excitement of the gallop. Michael sees smoke in the distance.*
*Nadia also sees the gray column rising up into the sky. It's on their side of the bank.*

NADIA: What could be on fire?

*They solemnly look at each other, as if they know. The river rages before them.*

STROGOFF: We must get across.

NADIA: It's too rough!

STROGOFF: Maybe farther down. Let's hurry!

*They ride hard again, down the shoreline, the mules' hooves kicking up spray.*
*They gallop for a couple of miles, then see a ferry boat on shore up ahead.*
*As they come, the Ferryman grabs his rifle, yet when he sees they are Russian he eases his weapon. He keeps it in his hand when Michael and Nadia ride near the dock.*
*A Younger Man, who helps steer a cart on, looks concerned at the approaching riders. But the Family on board has its own problems, trying to keep the two horses from spooking as well as keeping the bundles of books from falling. The cart carries a printing press wrapped in a tarp.*

YOUNG MAN: Who is coming?

FERRYMAN: We'll soon find out, son.

*Michael and Nadia halt before them.*

STROGOFF: Do you have room for us?

FERRYMAN: I'm not sure. Where are you bound?

STROGOFF: Omsk. As fast as we can get there.

*Nadia watches the Family with sympathy. The Ferryman carefully looks the New Travelers over.*

*Suddenly, the cart begins to slip. He goes to it quickly, holds it on while the Printer steers his horses. A wheel is slipping and may go off the dock. Michael climbs from his mount and helps. The cart slips smoothly onto the boat, and the Ferryman nods to Michael with gratitude.*

STROGOFF: Can we come with you?

FERRYMAN: Yes. But just you and the lady, not the mules. We're completely full, as you see.

*Michael takes out some coins, and hands them to the Ferryman.*

FERRYMAN: One other thing. We don't return. Did you see that smoke?

STROGOFF: Yes.

FERRYMAN: There are Tartars in the territory.

*Nadia and Michael quickly unsaddle their mules, then they lead them to the edge of the shore and set them free. The mules run down the shore with great beauty.*

*They climb on board the ferry, and the Young Man and Ferryman shove off with long poles. The ferryboat drifts into the current.*

## 76. ON THE RIVER IRTYCH - EXT/DAY

*The water rages but the Ferryman and his Son have the boat under control. Two Children play happily on the ferry near their wagon, a Boy and a Girl. Nadia watches them and smiles at Michael.*

NADIA: Sister and brother.

*But Michael's mind is elsewhere as he studies the passing terrain. The distant smoke has almost faded into the sky.*
*The Printer and his Wife secure most of their bundles. The river stretches very far, and all is quiet except for Children's laughter and the rush of current.*
*Nadia admires all the books and the fine printing press.*

NADIA: You have so many beautiful volumes!

WIFE: Thank you. Most of them are my husband's design.

PRINTER: Do you like to read?

NADIA: Very much!

PRINTER: 'A book is a world unto itself.' Don't you agree?

NADIA: I do.

*The Printer is wiping a small volume with his handkerchief. Nadia leans over to look at the wine red leather cover.*

NADIA: Holy Bible. Is that Latin?

PRINTER: This book is a rare edition. I always carry it
with me. This way I have the Prophets' wisdom
near whenever I'm in need. Do you read Latin?

NADIA: No, but I'd like to learn. My father knows Latin.
Also Greek.

*The Printer nods, understanding. He hands the book to
Nadia so she can look through it.*

*Michael listens to the river, his eyes peer at the empty shore.
He's obviously anxious.*

*The ferryboat rounds a bend in the river—and a Tartar
boat is waiting there, filled with Warriors! An arrow is let fly
and it catches the Printer in the neck. His Wife screams.*

*The boat heads toward the ferry. The Ferryman fires his
rifle, and a Tartar falls dead in the water. Michael also fires,
another Tartar meets the waves.*

*Arrows fill the sky. The Wife is struck in the stomach. An-
other catches the Young Man in the back as he frantically
poles. The Ferryman grabs his Son in sad rage. Nadia takes
the fallen rifle, checks it for powder, hands it to Michael. He
fires again, another Tartar dies. Then again with his pistol,
hitting his mark.*

*The Printer's Children are shocked at the sight of their
Dead Parents. Nadia grabs them and pulls them behind the
wagon, under covers. The horses are spooked now.*

*The Tartar boat is close. The Ferryman stands away from
his Dead Son, and in a fit of rage he fires his rifle...then
slings it at the coming boat. It hits a Warrior in the head.*

*But sudden rifle-shots find the Ferryman, his chest blossoming in blood. The ferryboat begins to spin in the current, and Michael grabs a pole.*

STROGOFF: Nadia! We must jump!

*But he sees that she protects the Children, holding them tightly to her in their fear. The horses begin to kick and stamp. Michael reaches for them—and a lance shaft grazes his head with such force he falls. The point enters the flank of the horse.*

*Michael struggles to stand, but as the ferryboat jerks in the current, he's knocked into the water. He sinks below the surface.*

NADIA: Nicholas!

*She screams and runs to the rear of the boat—but she cannot see him in the water. The Tartars throw a grappling hook into the bow. Nadia tries to rip it free, but the Warriors only laugh. Murga-ti leaps aboard and slaps the Woman to the deck.*

*The Tartars quickly untie the spooked horses from the wagon, then shove it into the river. The printing press sinks, but many books float atop the current.*

*Down river, Michael surfaces for an instant. His head bleeds from a huge gash. His eyes blur as he tries to focus on the boats far away. The current fights him, carries him—then he again goes under.*

క్ర

## 77. ON SHORE, NEAR OMSK - EXT/NIGHT

*A Hunchback wanders the shore-line, searching for valuable debris. He brushes off shells and places them in his sack. At a broken rowboat, he finds a rusted knife. This, too, he saves. Farther down the beach he sees something large, so he goes to investigate.*

*He is shocked to see a Man's body in the sand, but only a grunt comes from the Hunchback's mouth, no words. He squats near the body, rolls it over. Michael is unconscious, and his head still bleeds.*

*The Hunchback looks around carefully, but no one is in sight. He rummages through Michael's pockets and finds a purse with money. He finds the dispatch pouch. He opens it and stares in awe at the Imperial Seal. Quickly the Hunchback replaces everything, then feels Michael's neck for breathing.*

*With little effort, the Hunchback picks Michael up, slings him over his shoulder, then carries him down the dark beach.*

## 78. THE HUNCHBACK'S HUT - INT/NIGHT

*Michael lays on a cot, shivering with fever. The Hunchback rinses a rag in a bowl, then applies it to the Man's forehead. It doesn't seem to have any effect.*

*Michael is delirious. As he twists and turns on the pillow, sweat staining the cloth, he dreams of Nadia—*

## 78A. MONTAGE: MICHAEL'S DELIRIOUS FLASHBACKS

*Nadia walks toward him through tall grass…Nadia making love, her face glowing in the campfire…Nadia laughs with joy at dinner on the 'Caucasus'…. Nadia protects the children to her as the Tartars attack the ferryboat—*

## 78B. THE HUT, IN THE PRESENT

*Michael almost screams in sleep, and the Hunchback has to hold him down.*

## 79. HUNCHBACK'S HUT - INT/DAY

*Light streams in from the window, grazing Michael's eyes. He awakens and looks curiously around. The Hunchback grins. Michael reaches for his weapons, but they are no longer on him. The startled motion scares the Hunchback.*

STROGOFF: Who are you?

*The Hunchback points to himself, then takes a parchment and scratches a name with charcoal. SERKO.*

STROGOFF: You can't talk.

*Serko becomes solemn. He puts his hand over his mouth, shakes his head…then draws out his fingers and slashes at them with his palm.*

STROGOFF: I don't understand.

*The Hunchback repeats the slashing motion again and again until tears of anger fill his eyes. It becomes obvious to Michael now that someone has cut out the man's tongue.*

STROGOFF: Who did that to you? The Tartars?

*The Hunchback nods solemnly. Michael is sympathetic.*
*Michael tries to stand, but is dizzy. Serko hands him a small cracked piece of mirror, and Michael sees the gash in his head from the spear. He struggles to the window. Outside the hut is clutter: piles of old wood, fishnets, broken barrels. The riverbank. Michael stares at the sun glistening on the water.*

STROGOFF: There was a woman with me. Did you see her?

*Serko shakes his head.*

STROGOFF: How long have I been here?

*Serko holds up two fingers.*

STROGOFF: Two days? Damn!

*Michael notices an unused wooden sled out the window. It's covered over with crawling vines.*

STROGOFF: Do you have a horse? Or a mule?

*The Hunchback shakes his head, then makes a motion with his arm indicating the distance.*

STROGOFF: In Omsk?

*Serko nods energetically.*

STROGOFF: I have to get there. Can you help me Serko? I can pay a little bit.

*Serko smiles, then helps Michael stand. He places a wide fur hat on Michael, so the brim will cover his face.*
*They leave the hut and slowly make their way toward Omsk in the distance, Michael leaning on Serko for support.*


80. THE STREETS OF OMSK - EXT/DAY

*Warriors walk the streets. Russian deserters, Asian refugees, Tartars. Tents have been set up for the Renegade Army. The town has been taken over, and the People move about fearfully.*
*Serko and Michael come down an alley. Michael rests in pain against a wall. Serko is concerned. Blood seeps through a scarf over Michael's wound.*

STROGOFF: You're a good man, Serko. But I can manage now alone.

*The Hunchback, however, doesn't leave his side. They look at the passing Throng with distaste.*

*Suddenly, Michael sees a Group of Men in uniform, and a Woman. They ride with Tartars. Michael's eyes glare as he watches them go by: the Bohemian, Old Louis, Peter, Sangarre—and the Colonel who slapped him! Michael grits his teeth in anger.*

STROGOFF: Who is that officer?

*Murga-Ti rides beside the Colonel, and all Warriors stand respectfully.*

STROGOFF: Do you know him?

*Serko nods. He looks around for something to write with, finally finding a piece of coal. On the stone wall of the alley he writes ZUREVNO. Michael is shocked by this revelation.*

STROGOFF: My God!

*Michael stares hatefully until his Enemy is lost in the Crowd.*

STROGOFF: I must get to Irkutsk immediately! Serko, can people still purchase horses freely?

*The Hunchback nods.*

STROGOFF: My mother had a room above a tavern and stable. "Andrevsky's." Do you know it?

*The Hunchback shrugs, unsure.*

STROGOFF: Well then, I must hurry.

*He gives Serko some coins, but the Hunchback refuses to take the money. Michael forcefully stuffs it into Serko's pockets.*

STROGOFF: Please! You've been too good to me.

*There are so many Renegades in the street. Serko grabs his sleeve and signals for Michael to wait.*

STROGOFF: I don't understand.

*Suddenly Serko runs into the street alone. He begins to do a wild dance, circling clownishly, waving his arms. The Tartars and Russian Deserters laugh at him.*
*During this clever distraction, Michael pulls his hat low over his face and walks quickly across the street without anyone paying attention.*


## 81. ANDREVSKY'S, MARFA'S ROOM - INT/DAY

*Marfa Strogoff, an Elderly Woman, works upstairs near a window. Her hands expertly sew a quilt. Stacks of garments are on a table beside her. She looks out the window often and watches the street below.*
*There is a knock at her door. Andrevsky, a robust Older Man, comes in. He anxiously drops a stack of tattered Russian army uniforms on the table with the other goods.*

ANDREVSKY: Marfa! We need these repaired right away!

MARFA: I'm almost finished with this quilt, Ivan.

ANDREVSKY: You can go back to that later. Please, Marfa! The soldiers are waiting downstairs!

*Marfa looks at him in disgust.*

MARFA: If they're loyal soldiers then I'm a blue swan!

*Andrevsky smiles sarcastically.*

ANDREVSKY: Well, they pay!

MARFA: Dear Ivan, you should be worrying about other things.

*Andrevsky shrugs, then leaves. The Old Woman begins stitching up the uniforms. Her hands are deft and fast. Although the work is menial, she is dignified.*
*Suddenly she pricks her finger.*

MARFA: Ouch!

*She stands, sucking on the tiny wound. She kicks the uniforms in disgust.*

MARFA: Renegade scum!

*From a small kettle she pours herself some tea, sips it, stares lovingly at a small painting in an old frame: a Bear-Hunter with a hide, standing beside a Young Boy…obviously Michael and his Father.*

*Marfa's eyes go sad…but then they shift to the window again. She sees a Man with a fur hat down at the stable. For some reason she keeps staring, and as the Man pays Andrevsky for a horse, his face tilts up. She recognizes him immediately.*

MARFA: Michael?

*She knocks frantically at the window pane.*

MARFA: My son!

*The Man with the horse can't hear her, so she quickly hurries from her room.*

## 82. THE TAVERN, DOWNSTAIRS - INT/DAY

*She bumps into People at the bar, almost spilling the Bohemian's ale. Sangarre is there, also.*

BOHEMIAN: Be careful, woman!

MARFA: I'm sorry! But my son is here!

*She runs outside. Sangarre and the Bohemian watch her curiously.*

BOHEMIAN: If her son is fighting age, we should enlist him.

# 83. THE STREET, NEAR THE BARN - EXT/DAY

*Michael leads the horse away, but Marfa is running toward him. She calls out desperately.*

MARFA: Michael! Michael Strogoff!

*Michael slowly turns, but his face is grim, his eyes cold.*

STROGOFF: Excuse me?

MARFA: Oh, Michael! It's Marfa!

*Marfa approaches, but Michael holds out his arm to stop her.*

STROGOFF: I'm sorry, Madame. You must be mistaken.

*Through the tavern window, Sangarre watches the strange confrontation. Michael seems familiar to her.*
*Marfa is astonished by the rejection.*

MARFA: Son? Are you ill? It's me!

STROGOFF: You have the wrong man.

*Tears fill Marfa's eyes. Michael looks around to see if they're being overheard.*

MARFA: Please! Michael? Don't you think I know my own child!

*Michael very subtly nods, but then his voice is again raised.*

STROGOFF: Madame, you are confused.

*But he smiles slightly, and Marfa understands. She whispers under her breath.*

MARFA: It's dangerous here...take me with you.

*Michael curtly nods, then shifts his eyes directly out of town. As he turns his horse, he whispers also.*

STROGOFF: Hurry! I can't wait, Mother!

*Then, as he leaves her, he motions dramatically as if to wave her away.*

STROGOFF: You're a crazy woman! I feel sorry for you!

*She watches him lead the horse down the street, then quickly goes back to the tavern. Sangarre has seen it all from the window.*

## 84. THE TAVERN - INT/DAY

*Marfa passes swiftly by Andrevsky on her way back upstairs.*

ANDREVSKY: Marfa, what's wrong? Are you ill?

MARFA: No, Ivan. It's just that...I thought I saw my son
         outside.

ANDREVSKY: Michael? I haven't seen him since he was a small lad! Don't know if I'd even recognize him. Isn't he in Moscow?

MARFA: Yes, of course he is!

*Marfa hurries upstairs. Andrevsky fills more mugs of ale and carries them to the Bohemian and Sangarre.*

SANGARRE: Will your friend be all right?

ANDREVSKY: Yes, I think so. She's a fine worker. But now that winter's upon us, her old bones are taking the strain.

SANGARRE: Is her son dead? Is that why she went a little crazy?

ANDREVSKY: No...as far as I know her son still lives. He's posted in Moscow.

SANGARRE: What does he do there?

ANDREVSKY: He's with the Imperial Guard. In the Courier service, I believe.

*The Bohemian's mug of ale stops midway to his mouth. Sangarre catches her breath, and the Two Traitors stare at each other hard.*

## 85. MARFA'S ROOM UPSTAIRS - INT/DAY

*As quickly as she can, Marfa is packing. She stuffs clothes into a carpetbag, all the while anxiously looking through the window. She sees Michael and the horse disappear at the farthest edge of town.*

*She anxiously finishes, then slips the painting in her bag.*

*Suddenly her door bursts open! Sangarre, the Bohemian, and Peter stand there. Peter's rifle is trained on the Old Woman.*

PETER: Marfa Strogoff?

MARFA: Yes?

PETER: You are commanded to come with us immediately!

*The Two Men grab the Old Woman and roughly push her out the door. Sangarre smiles viciously and retrieves the carpet bag which was dropped.*

## 86. THE FAR EDGE OF TOWN, A SIDE STREET EXT/DUSK

*Michael waits, his horse's reins held ready. He is anxious. No one is at this corner. The noise from town is faint, the steppes sprawl behind him.*

*Michael is concerned. He thinks of the Czar's orders, and in his mind the words echo—*

## 86a. FLASHBACK: THE CZAR'S CHAMBERS

*Alexander's face is stern and earnest.*

CZAR ALEXANDER: Reveal yourself to no one! Not even
your own mother will know your identity. Mother
Russia is your only parent....

## 86b. ON THE STREET

*Michael mounts the horse and stares toward town one last
time. The sun is about to set. He whispers sadly.*

MICHAEL: Forgive me, Mother!

*He spurs his horse and gallops away toward the steppes.*

ভৎ

## 87. CITY HALL, INNER COURTYARD - EXT/DUSK

*The Mayor of Omsk and several Councilmen have been shoved
against a stone wall with their hands tied behind them. Tartars and Deserters stand with weapons loaded and ready for
the execution. Zurevno is in command and about to give the
signal.*

ZUREVNO: Gentlemen, as the sun sets around us, so will
your lives sink from memory. But I hope you appreciate that I'm allowing you an honorable

soldier's death. A death with dignity, that I'm sure none of you truly deserve.

*The Mayor stands tall and spits at the Colonel.*

MAYOR: Zurevno! You are a coward and traitor! I pray that you will burn in Hell!

*The Colonel raises his arm. Rifles blaze, arrows fly. The Prisoners fall, blood splatters on the wall and on some flowers growing near.*

*Zurevno walks over to inspect. Among the bloody flowers he finds one that is clean. He picks it, sniffs, then tosses it onto the Mayor's stiff body.*

## 88. MAYOR'S OFFICE - INT/NIGHT

*Zurevno leans over an exquisite chess board with ornate ivory pieces. He is playing a serious game with himself. He concentrates so hard he barely hears the knock on the door.*

ZUREVNO: Yes! Enter!

*Sangarre and Old Louis come in, but Zurevno immediately holds up his hand to stop them from speaking.*

SANGARRE: This is important, Victor!

*But the Colonel shakes his head no. He contemplates the black bishop on the white knight...then makes his move.*

SANGARRE: Victor ...

ZUREVNO: My love, do you appreciate the beauty of this
game? The elegance of craftsmanship and
thought?

SANGARRE: We have a captive. You should talk to this
woman.

*Peter and the Bohemian bring in Marfa. They have tied
the Old Woman's hands.*
*Sangarre places the carpetbag on Zurevno's desk and whis-
pers to him.*

SANGARRE: We caught her trying to join her son, trying
to leave Omsk with him.

ZUREVNO: So?

SANGARRE: Do you remember the talk of the courier?

ZUREVNO: Yes ...

SANGARRE: This is his mother! The man must have just
been here spying for the Czar!

*Finally Zurevno takes an interest. He stares at Marfa.*

ZUREVNO: Your name?

MARFA: Marfa Strogoff.

ZUREVNO: Where is your husband?

MARFA: He is in Heaven.

*Zurevno smirks. He empties her carpet-bag and notices the painting.*

ZUREVNO: You have a son?

MARFA: Yes.

ZUREVNO: His name?

MARFA: Michael.

ZUREVNO: Is he in heaven, also?

MARFA: No. He's in Moscow.

ZUREVNO: What does he do there?

MARFA: He's in the Imperial Guard.

ZUREVNO: I see. What are his specific duties?

*Marfa is silent. Sangarre grabs the Old Woman's bound hands and twists so Marfa is forced down to the floor. The ropes cut into her wrists. Sangarre keeps twisting. Marfa's arms burn so much the skin bleeds.*

ZUREVNO: What are Michael Strogoff's specific duties, madame?

MARFA:...courier....

*She's in great pain so the word barely emerges.*
*The Colonel signals for Sangarre to let Marfa up. Tears flow from the Old Woman's eyes, yet she faces Zurevno with dignity.*

MARFA: My son...Michael...is a courier for the Czar!

*Zurevno smiles with satisfaction.*

ZUREVNO: When did you last see your son?

MARFA: Almost four years ago.

SANGARRE: She's lying! He was here in Omsk, today!

ZUREVNO: Is this true, Marfa?

MARFA: No, it is not! As I said, I haven't seen him in four years at least!

SANGARRE: Then who was the man you spoke to in the street? The man you were going to meet...who you called to as your son!

MARFA: He was a stranger. I admit that he looked like Michael. But I was wrong.

ZUREVNO: Then why were you going off with him?

BOHEMIAN: Perhaps so she could become his dear lover.

*Everyone laughs. Marfa is humiliated. Zurevno waves for quiet.*

ZUREVNO: So this young man of yours was not Michael Strogoff, the Czar's brave and fearless courier?

MARFA: No.

ZUREVNO: Old Woman, we could torture you until you confess the truth?

*Fear crosses Marfa's face. Zurevno is solemn, his eyes gleaming with malice.*

ZUREVNO: Now, once again—where is your son?

MARFA: Moscow.

*Zurevno cannot hold his anger.*

ZUREVNO: Take her out of my sight!

*Peter and the Bohemian lead Marfa from the room.*

SANGARRE: This worries me, Victor.

ZUREVNO: Alert our troops to be on the look-out for this courier.

SANGARRE: What about the Old Woman?

ZUREVNO: I know how to make the old witch confess!

*Sangarre comes close to him and holds him, kisses him. But Zurevno's thoughts are elsewhere.*

ZUREVNO: I must visit our guest.

*He breaks from her, and goes out the door. She stiffens, then goes to the window and looks down into the courtyard. Peter and the Bohemian steer the Old Woman, who keeps trying to struggle free.*

## 89. THE PRISON BARN - INT/NIGHT

*The doors open and Marfa is shoved in by Peter and the Bohemian. Two large Guards lead her toward Other Women in the corner, sitting on the hay.*

BOHEMIAN: Watch her carefully.

GUARD: Yes, sir.

*The Guard salutes. The door is closed. It's dank and dark in there. It seems like a Hundred Women and Children fill the barn. There are Female Guards, also. Everyone is tense and afraid.*

*In a corner, Nadia has seen Marfa carried in. She watches with sympathy. Nadia is dirty and wet. Her face bleeds from scratches, but her eyes are hard.*

*Marfa is handed a ragged blanket. She finds room on the straw next to a Mother nursing a Baby.*

*The door opens again. Two Women bring in a large kettle. A Guard starts to dish up the filthy soup.*

GUARD: Fall in line if you want to eat!

*The Women wearily stand. Soup is handed to them in wooden bowls. They hungrily slurp it up. Marfa takes hers and sits quietly. When it's Nadia's turn, she stares at the liquid with disgust.*

NADIA: What's in this?

GUARD: None of your concern. But it'll keep you healthy, darling.

*Other Guards snicker. Nadia throws the bowl against the wall, the soup splattering. She goes back to her lonely corner. The Guards laugh more. Marfa takes note of the Younger Woman's defiance.*

## 90. CITY HALL, CELLAR DUNGEON - INT/NIGHT

*Zurevno opens the door. Jolivet sits behind bars, reading a small book with a red leather cover. He doesn't look toward the Colonel, even as they speak.*

ZUREVNO: I apologize for these unfortunate accommodations, Monsieur.

JOLIVET: I'm well aware of your motivations, Colonel Gorlov. But I assure you, I'm not a spy. The politics of your country are not my concern.

ZUREVNO: I have misled you. My name is Victor
          Zurevno.

JOLIVET: I thought as much. I'm not a fool, sir. To quote
          Ecclesiastes: "There is an evil in all that is done
          under the sun, and there is one fate for all men.
          Furthermore, the hearts of the sons of men are
          full of evil, and insanity is in their hearts through-
          out their lives. They go to the dead—"

*Zurevno reaches through the bars and grabs the Bible from
Jolivet's hands. It's the Dead Printer's edition.*

ZUREVNO: I thought you were an intelligent man.

JOLIVET: Your ally, Chief Murga-Ti, gave me that as a
          gift of good faith. It seems he found it in the river,
          floating in the sun like a miracle. It's all Latin,
          you see.

ZUREVNO: I don't give a damn.

*Jolivet holds up his sketching paper to show his portrait of
Murga-Ti.*

JOLIVET: Quite a good likeness, don't you think? I espe-
          cially care for the tortuous gleam in the eyes and
          the barbaric blood-lust that seems to twist the lips.

*Zurevno laughs. He opens the cell door.*

ZUREVNO: You are free.

*Jolivet doesn't move.*

JOLIVET: I think I would rather stay. There is too much
        killing going on outside for my tastes.

ZUREVNO: There is a condition to your release.

JOLIVET: I'm sure.

ZUREVNO: Let's call it a pact. Between two intelligent
        gentlemen of the world.

*He hands the Bible back to the Journalist.*

ZUREVNO: I want you to write my story. I will tell you
        the truth of my struggle, including the history of
        my family…and you will write it very eloquently
        to make sure my words reach your readers all
        across Europe.

JOLIVET: I'm a journalist, not a propagandist!

ZUREVNO: What I have to say is important. Will you do
        it? The price is your freedom.

JOLIVET: Then I have no choice.

ZUREVNO: Few of us actually do, Monsieur Jolivet.

*Zurevno pulls up a chair and indicates that Jolivet should take up his paper and pencil. Then the Colonel begins to explain.*

ZUREVNO: There are men who are special, they're born this way. I always knew I'd be a fine soldier. I even had a head for strategy as a young boy staging snowball fights with my friends. I always knew I'd someday make history and that all of Russia would admire my name. My task was to grasp control over the situations I was involved in....

*Jolivet scribbles as fast as he can, and his irritation slowly turns into fascination as Zurevno rambles on.*

JOLIVET'S NARRATION [*voice-over*]: "I listened that night for several hours, and it was certainly one of the strangest biographies I'd ever heard. He told me of his father, a controversial statesman who had been mysteriously assassinated after drafting a treaty with Germany. Of his sad mother who died giving birth to him. Of his two older brothers, one a crippled consumptive who had a great gift for music. The other, an actor, was killed in front of their house by a runaway carriage. He talked of his years of excellence at the military academy, ending in disgrace when he was expelled for dueling with one of his teachers, nearly killing the man with a dagger. His military career, accomplishing remarkable feats on the battle-field but refusing to accept the simplest disciplinary

commands from his superiors…and on and on. I
wrote as fast as I could because my life depended
on it. Yet I knew that my life depended even more
on my escape from this madman…"

## 91. PRISON BARN - INT/NIGHT

*As the door opens, torchlight streaks across the floor, causing
most of the Women to awaken. Murga-Ti stands at the door
with some Guards. Nadia watches as he enters.*

*The Tartar begins to inspect certain Women, staring at
them closely under the torches. He points to one, an Asian
beauty, and the Guard with the whip lifts her. He continues
his search. Nadia tries to shrink deep into her corner.*

*Another Woman is taken, also Asian with a pretty face
and figure. Murga-Ti wanders through the Women, stepping
over them, heading to where Nadia hides.*

*The torch illuminates her face. Murga-Ti smiles.*

MURGA-TI: You.

*The Guards start to lift Nadia to her feet, but she fights.
She bites one Guard's hand. He moves to strike her, but Murga-
Ti stops him.*

MURGA-TI: This one is a wildcat. All the better.

*They take the Three Women out. Marfa has seen, but when
the door is slammed, darkness again covers her face.*

## 92. MURGA-TI'S TENT - INT/NIGHT

*The Tartar sits on pillows surrounded by golden candlelight. He drinks wine and sucks on his opium pipe, the smoke rising to the ceiling in a haze. In a corner, a Musician plays a wooden flute. The music is soothing, somber.*

*Colonel Zurevno enters the tent. He carries the ornate chess set. Bowing, he sits, then offers the board to the Tartar.*

ZUREVNO: I have brought this gift for you, Murga-Ti.

*The Tartar picks up the queen, then the bishop, admiring them.*

MURGA-TI: It is most beautiful. I thank you, Colonel. I do not play chess, but Feofar Khan does. Quite well.

ZUREVNO: So now you can join him, with my gracious compliments.

MURGA-TI: I will do so.

*The Tartar pours Zurevno a chalice of wine. He lights the opium pipe and passes it over. The Colonel indulges.*

MURGA-TI: You have impressed us, Colonel. We have begun to trust you.

ZUREVNO: Thank you.

MURGA-TI: I believe our alliance will be a great thing.

ZUREVNO: I, also, believe this.

MURGA-TI: I leave tomorrow to join the Khan. What
            are your plans?

ZUREVNO: If it's agreeable, we should meet at the Khan's
            camp in four days. I expect to pick up more men
            at Tobsk. I already have scouts there. The city is
            vulnerable.

MURGA-TI: Excellent! Your army is gaining strength.

*Murga-Ti whispers to the Musician, then he leaves the
tent.*
*The Tartar lights another pipe, sucks on it, passes it to
Zurevno.*

MURGA-TI: I have prepared a special entertainment for
            us tonight. I hope you enjoy it.

ZUREVNO: I'm sure I will.

*The Musician returns, sits, but now begins to play a little
drum quietly. Several Guards enter, pushing the three Women
Prisoners. They have been dressed in skimpy veiled costumes,
Nadia also. Zurevno stares at her.*

MURGA-TI: My ladies, you have been chosen for a most
            wonderful task tonight. You will dance in honor

of Colonel Zurevno's victory over this town. If you perform well, this will be a sweet evening for you. You will be allowed to eat with us until you are full, and possibly keep me company on my journey to join our master, the Khan.

*Murga-Ti signals to a Guard, who pours three chalices of wine. He takes them to the Women. The Two Asians drink thirstily, but Nadia refuses. The Guard with the whip stares angrily.*

MURGA-TI: I have personally chosen the three of you because of your exceptional beauty. I'm sure none of you will disappoint us.

*He eats some grapes. The Women stare hungrily at the food, but suddenly the drum beat gets louder. Murga-Ti signals for the Women to begin.*

*The rhythm is steady, moody and erotic. Hesitantly, the Two Asian Women begin to move. They sway shyly, solemnly. Murga-Ti is enthralled. Nadia stands defiantly still. Zurevno can't take his eyes from her.*

*The drum becomes more rapid, frenetic. The two Asians move in a more sensual way. The Tartar laughs and claps his hands. The Women smile. They shimmy, their bodies begin to sweat. Nadia is disgusted.*

*Murga-Ti eats more grapes, then throws some at the Women. They scoop them off the floor and gobble them down. He throws figs at them, they grab for this, too. They continue to dance. Murga-Ti notices how closely Zurevno studies Nadia.*

MURGA-TI: She will be my present to you, Colonel.

*Murga-Ti signals for the Asian women to join him. He gives them more wine. The Musician stops drumming and plays his flute again. Zurevno approaches Nadia.*

ZUREVNO: I know you. What is your name?

NADIA: Nadia Fedor.

ZUREVNO: Where have we met?

NADIA: I don't know.

ZUREVNO: Why don't you dance?

NADIA: Because I'm not a fool.

ZUREVNO: No, but you are an exquisite woman.

NADIA: And you are a traitor, Colonel!

*Zurevno smiles, touches her hair, then her bare shoulder...and Nadia suddenly spits in his face. Murga-Ti laughs. Zurevno is humiliated, so he signals to the Guards. They grab Nadia, and the Guard with the whip smirks. Zurevno takes the weapon from him. Nadia struggles, but she can't possibly escape from these large Men.*

ZUREVNO: Bind her!

*Murga-Ti hands a Woman his pipe. She smokes. Then the Other does, also. They sit beside him on his pillows.*

*Nadia's hands are bound tightly in front of her. Zurevno points to the large center tent-post, so the Guards stretch her arms above her head and tie her.*

*Murga-Ti begins to fondle one of the Women, who's now dazed by the drink and opium.*

*Zurevno steps close to Nadia.*

ZUREVNO: You have very fine skin.

*Then he rips her clothes away, exposing her bare back. He cracks the whip. It flies across the air and bites into Nadia's flesh. She grits her teeth in pain, but does not cry out. Zurevno flogs her again and again. Blood flows where the whip cuts her. He doesn't stop until a weak whimper comes from Nadia's mouth.*

*Her back is covered with blood. She shivers, her eyes are blurry with tears. They suddenly roll back as she sinks into unconsciousness.*

*Murga-Ti smiles as he has his pleasure with both Women.*

## 93. ZUREVNO'S CHAMBERS - INT/NIGHT

*The Colonel orders the Guards to lay Nadia on his bed. The Woman moans.*

*Her eyes open with pain as the wounds brush the sheets. Zurevno unfastens his belt, and begins to rape her. She tries wearily to fight him off, but she's too weak.*

## 93a. OUTSIDE HIS DOOR

*Sangarre stands in the shadows, listening, her face grim with anger.*

## 94. PRISON BARN - INT/NIGHT - LATER

*The Guards bring in Nadia and lower her to the straw near Marfa. Clothes are thrown at her. A Female Guard stares at the wounds with sympathy.*

*Marfa stares at the hurt Woman. She inspects the wounds. The Female Guard lights a lamp, then hands Marfa some oil and bandages.*

*Marfa doctors Nadia, spreading the oil evenly across her back. She wraps her with bandages.*

*Soft groans of pain come from Nadia, and her eyes are filled with rage.*

∽

## 95. ACROSS THE STEPPES - EXT/NIGHT

*There's a low full moon. Michael gallops across its face.*

*He reaches a stream and stops to rest. The moon is reflected. For an instant, Nadia's face seems to appear...her long hair like seaweed, her expression that of drowned death.*

*Tears fill Michael's eyes.*

*Then he kicks the horse, and they gallop across the stream, the hooves shattering the ripples.*

## 96. A SWAMP - EXT/DAY

*Weary, and exhausted, Michael walks the horse through the deep mud. Hundreds of mosquitoes attack them, bite their faces, irritate the horse's ears and nose and eyes. Michael swats them away, but it does no good.*

*Suddenly the horse slips and falls. He can't rise again. It's quicksand! Michael pulls with all his might on the reins.*

*The horse struggles, rises to the bank, then slips again. Michael keeps pulling. He's close to a tree. He wraps the reins around its trunk and pulls.*

STROGOFF: Don't die this way…!

*The horse regains its footing and pulls itself free.*

## 97. A CORNFIELD - EXT/DAY

*They walk through the tall stalks. The horse eats the dried-up shucks, Michael chews on kernels and drinks from a skin canteen. The sun is hot. At the edge of the field he sees smoke.*

*He mounts and rides fast through the field. He sees a house smoldering. Michael slows the horse and draws his pistol. He dismounts to investigate.*

*He cannot see anyone. The smoke is thick. He walks silently. The smoke clears, and he sees a head in the earth.*

*It's a Man, his eyes closed, his face bloody. He's been buried to the neck. Michael goes closer…suddenly the eyes open. But they stare forward as if seeing nothing.*

*The Man's lips move. Michael stoops down to listen to the whispering. He tries giving him water from the skin.*

MAN: Kill me....

STROGOFF: Did the Tartars do this?

*The Man's eyes try to find Michael. His lips are cracked with heat, his face is blistered. The pitiful voice is strained.*

MAN: Please...mercy....

*Michael moves behind his head and draws his pistol. He hesitates, but above are vultures circling in the sky, their wings dark against the sun.*

*His face grim with pity and disgust, Michael pulls the trigger, ending the Man's torment.*


## 98. A FOREST - EXT/NIGHT

*Michael trots his horse through the trees. Up ahead he sees circles of light. He dismounts and walks the horse quietly. As they get closer the lights grow brighter.*

*It's a campfire and torches. Tying the horse to a branch, he crawls through the grass. He hears Men's voices, laughter. He sees Tartars and Russian deserters. They drink and eat around the fire.*

RUSSIAN #1: I know this territory well. You listen to me and we'll do fine.

TARTAR #2: Then where could a man hide?

RUSSIAN #1: Anywhere! Everywhere!

*They all laugh and drink some more. Michael watches carefully.*

TARTAR #2: If he's around here, he can't get by us. I know, yet I am not from this place.

RUSSIAN #1: Then why are you so sure?

*The Tartar rips meat with his teeth from his huge knife, then throws the blade into a tree. There's more laughter from the Warriors.*

RUSSIAN #1: We must keep searching. In the morning we will find him.

RUSSIAN #2: One man. Why such a special hunt?

RUSSIAN #1: Colonel Zurevno orders it.

TARTAR #1: If he comes from this region, then he will know the area as well as we do.

RUSSIAN #1: No. He's from Moscow. That city will have ruined him, dulled his senses. I've been there. I know. You go soft.

RUSSIAN #2: But couriers are smart. And they make it their business to ride fast and not be seen.

RUSSIAN #1: He was a fool, then. But that Old Woman,
his mother…they say she was a tough one.

*Michael suddenly realizes they're talking about him, and
about Marfa!*

TARTAR #2: I do not care about spies and old women
tonight. A young woman, though, would find my
interest.

*The Tartar grabs his crotch, and they all laugh again.*

TARTAR #1: My friend, forgive me…but I was led to
believe your only love was your horse!

TARTAR #2: A much different kind of ride. But more
reliable and less trouble!

*In the glow of the firelight, Michael sees the horses a short
distance away in a thicket. The Tartar goes over to them with
scraps from the meal.*

*The Tartar is feeding the horses affectionately. He doesn't
see or hear Michael when he's grabbed from behind. Michael's
knife slices across his throat. The Tartar falls in his blood. The
horses whinny. Michael quickly cuts them loose, one-by-one
down the line. As the horses start running wildly, so does he.*

*The horses head for the camp. The Warriors are startled by
the stampede. Guns are fired in fear, which spook the horses
even more. The Russian keeps his head and is able to catch his
horse. As he quiets it, he sees Michael running in the shadows.*

*The Russian yells to his partners.*

RUSSIAN #1: I see him!

## 99. THE FOREST TRAIL - EXT/NIGHT

*Michael rides fast, the Warriors in pursuit. They fire their guns, just missing him in the dark. The trees shield him and bullets ricochet from the limbs near his head.*

*He sees torches moving rapidly behind him. He hears angry shouting.*

*Suddenly, the horse rears up, and Michael is nearly thrown. They've reached the edge of a ravine above a river!*

*Michael is unsure how far below the water is. Suddenly a bullet strikes the horse in the neck. It falls, pulling Michael down with it. Michael jumps free, but the animal is dead.*

*More shots go over his head and into the water. The current is forceful. The carcass begins to slide down the slope toward the water.*

*Without thinking, Michael grabs on.*

## 100. THE RIVER - EXT/NIGHT

*The carcass and Man land in the water. Michael climbs onto the horse's belly and it floats!*

*The Warriors have reached the shore. They keep firing, but darkness hinders their aim. Michael goes underwater, but keeps hanging onto the horse's legs. The Warriors can't find him at all. When the carcass floats far enough downriver, he comes up for air. He wipes water from his eyes and sees the tiny light from their torches recede in the distance.*

## 101. THE RIVER - EXT/NIGHT

*For the rest of the night, Michael lays on top of the horse as the river carries him away.*

ल

## 102. ON SHORE, A WOODLAND - EXT/DAY

*Michael sleeps, and the horse carcass runs aground. Flies swarm around it. Michael awakens from the stench…and from a loud booming noise in the distance.*

*He slips into the water and rinses his sleepy eyes. He steps onto dry land. The carcass is again taken by the current and floats away.*

*He pulls out the dispatch pouch. The parchment is damp, but the seal is intact. He heads through the trees toward the noise.*

*The booming gains in intensity. Michael knows this sound!*

*He runs as fast as he can, stumbles to the ground, picks himself up and continues on.*

*He reaches a clearing. In the distance, Tobsk stands on the far steppes. Flames, smoke, and dust surround the area.*

*Suddenly, a Troop of Tartars head toward him. The dust is protective, so he ducks back in the trees. They pass, and there's more cannon sounds.*

*He runs back to the river.*

*He keeps along the shore, fear driving him on.*

## 103. MONTAGE:

*He runs, sometimes hiding from patrols. The cannon fire has faded, all he hears is his own strained breathing and exertion.*

## 104. ALONG THE RIVERBANK - EXT/DAY

*Clouds cover the sky. Snow begins to fall. Michael shivers with chill. He sits on a rock to rest. He shivers. He splatters water on his face and drinks.*

*Looking up, he sees the horse carcass in the water up ahead. It's a wonderment. It's caught against a dock across the river. He jumps in and swims toward it.*

## 105. THE DOCK - EXT/DAY

*He pulls himself up. There's a small rowboat stuck between the bloated carcass and the dock. Michael climbs in and takes up the oars.*

*He shoves off from the dead animal and rows down the river.*

ও

## 106. THE RIVER, NEAR KOLYVAN - EXT/DAY

*More snow falls. Michael rows hard. The town of Kolyvan seems quiet up ahead. There are peaceful hills, stately church domes.*

*Michael docks the boat on shore.*

*Suddenly, the quiet is shattered by more cannon fire. The trees shake with the tremor. Michael can't see where the guns come from.*

*There's a small building up ahead. He moves toward it.*

## 107. TELEGRAPH OFFICE - EXT/DAY

*Michael sees the wires and the pole still standing.*

STROGOFF: A miracle …

*A single horse stands outside the building. From inside he hears the tapping of a message and a Familiar Voice. Michael looks in the window.*

## 108. TELEGRAPH OFFICE - INT/DAY

*Jolivet mumbles to himself as he rapidly works the transmitting device. The Journalist is dirty, unshaven, and he seems nearly shell-shocked.*

JOLIVET: "In the poppy field we lay/ As the sun bursts across the sky/ Yet above our heads are angels/ Laughing at our folly and fate—"

*He pauses, and laughs to himself. Michael whispers desperately to him.*

STROGOFF: Jolivet!

*The Journalist spins around nervously.*

JOLIVET: Monsieur Korpanoff, hello! Please sit. I'm composing my poem to Paris and it's almost done.

*More cannon fire shocks Michael, and dust from the ceiling falls on them. Jolivet returns to the telegraph.*

JOLIVET: "Into our hearts go mad songs/ The ringing of which we bear/ Yet only our sweet angels keep smiling/ For—"

*He can't find the words. Michael is frantic.*

STROGOFF: Jolivet, damn it!

JOLIVET: "For the rest of us are stained with tears!"

*He finishes tapping with a flourish.*

STROGOFF: What are you doing?

JOLIVET: Sending my last message before the world falls completely apart.

*Michael pulls Jolivet from the chair and sits in his place at the machine.*

STROGOFF: I need to send one, also. Then we'll leave together on your horse.

*Jolivet nods and sits on a bench against the wall. More cannon fire frightens the horse, which pulls at the hitching-post. Jolivet hushes it.*

STROGOFF: If I can reach Irkutsk…warn the Grand Duke….

*Suddenly a shell hits the building and takes out a wall! The machine goes dead. Boards rain down on them. Then another shell explodes the roof. The building is on fire! The blast has knocked the Men to the floor.*

*Michael climbs to his feet and helps Jolivet. They cough in the smoke and dust, then struggle outside.*

## 109. REMAINS OF TELEGRAPH OFFICE - EXT/DAY

*The building is a wrecked shambles. The horse stands alive. As Michael begins to lift Jolivet onto the animal, a Troop of Tartars ride up. There are so many Warriors, they quickly surround the Men. Rifles and cross-bows are aimed to kill.*

*Michael raises his hands in grim surrender. Warriors dismount and tie his hands, also Jolivet's. They loop thick ropes around their necks and lead them away…while the building burns behind them.*

☙

## 110. THE STEPPES - EXT/DUSK

*Snow falls on the long line of hundreds of Male Captives. They walk with ropes looped around their necks, each connected to the man in front and behind. They're beaten and bloody, covered with grime. The Wounded are carried by the healthier ones.*

*Tartar Guards ride up and down the column. Soldiers surround the Captives on all sides, so there's no possibility of escape.*

*Michael is attached to Jolivet. He watches the Tartars carefully. The Journalist, however, closes his eyes with exhaustion. This forces Michael to nearly carry him along.*

*They reach a plateau, and looking down they see the many tents of the Tartar camp. Both awe and great fear fills the eyes of the Men.*

## 111. THE TARTAR CAMP - EXT/NIGHT

*The Men are held in a huge fenced corral. Guards are posted on the periphery. Snow falls steadily on the few fires the Captives are allowed. They huddle close to keep warm, sometimes shoving each other angrily.*

*Jolivet and Michael sit together.*

JOLIVET: He wanted me to write his biography. But I wouldn't. So I escaped.

STROGOFF: What are you talking about?

JOLIVET: He ordered me to write a book about him. He was going to lock me up like a eunuch until I did it. But I fooled him.

*Michael just stares at him. Another Captive, Mikhail, shakes his head at this apparent madness.*

JOLIVET: Zurevno.

*Michael pokes a stick angrily at the fire.*

STROGOFF: These are not his troops, are they?

JOLIVET: Who can tell?

MIKHAIL: They are not. Zurevno is behind us. But he's coming!

*The Guards and other Warriors burst into the corral. They start to shove the Captives into formation.*

TARTAR CHIEF: Line up! Quickly!

*The Captives struggle weakly to do this. When lines are orderly, the Tartar Chief walks slowly down the columns and singles out every Fifth Man. Behind him, Guards haul the chosen ones away.*

*The Men are so tired and beaten they seldom resist. A sack is thrown into the Crowd of Captives. Moldy bread falls out, but the Men scramble for it. The Tartars laugh.*

*Michael, Jolivet, and Mikhail eat by the fire. In the distance, they hear hammering noises...and then screams of pain.*

JOLIVET: What is happening to them?

STROGOFF: I don't know.

*There is more hammering farther away, and more screams of pain. There is a sad, dark look in Mikhail's eyes.*

MIKHAIL: They are being crucified.

*Michael and Jolivet stare at him in horror.*

## 112. ON A NEARBY HILL

*Men nailed to crosses are lifted from the ground into the air. They stand in silhouette against the sky, twisting in agony until they are dead.*

&

## 113. THE STEPPES - EXT/DAY

*A long column of Women Captives, some carrying Children, trudge through the snow. When someone falls, they are left to die.*

*Zurevno's Army guards the Women. Sangarre and the Bohemian ride along, watching them carefully. The Bohemian yells for the Captives to keep moving. Sangarre keeps a hateful eye on Nadia, who silently walks beside Marfa.*

*Peter rides across the plateau toward Zurevno, who is at the head of the column. Peter rears in his horse excitedly, then points.*

PETER: Over that rise, Colonel. They're expecting us in glory.

*Zurevno straightens his jacket and crooks his cap. His eyes glisten with delight. He anxiously spurs his horse.*

*The column continues on...and the first strange sight is the long rows of Crucified Men leading into the Tartar camp. The crosses decorate both sides of the road. The Women stare at the dead with terror and sadness as they walk by. Even Zurevno finds it grim.*

## 114. THE TARTAR CAMP - EXT/DAY

*Hundreds of tents lay before them. Tartar Warriors line the road where the crosses end. Zurevno rides proudly by. He sees Male Prisoners in a far corral, their pitiful faces staring—*

*And Michael watches Zurevno, his eyes seething with worry and hatred.*

JOLIVET: That's him! A maniac! If he finds me here I'll be nailed to one of those crosses!

## 114a. CENTRAL PLAZA - EXT/DAY

*Zurevno rides with dignity. Banners fill the air as he approaches the tent of Feofar Khan. The Khan sits on an ornate throne of hides and jewels. He wears golden armor and feathers, more jewels in his long hair. Murga-Ti stands to one side, Roola to the other.*

*The Colonel dismounts, approaches, then bows.*

FEOFAR KHAN: Colonel Zurevno! It is our very great
   pleasure to have you.

ZUREVNO: Feofar Khan!

*Murga-Ti fills two large chalices with red wine. He holds
them out ritualistically. Roola steps forward, says a silent prayer
over them, and sprinkles the chalices with herbs and ground
peppers. Then Murga-Ti hands both cups to the Khan. He
then keeps one and hands the other to Zurevno.*

*The Khan dramatically links his drinking arm with
Zurevno's.*

FEOFAR KHAN: This is the Russian way, is it not?

ZUREVNO: Yes, Sire.

*The Khan laughs. They both drink, their eyes glued to the
other until the chalices are completely drained. The Warriors
then yell with enthusiastic approval, the Crowd going wild.*


115. A FIELD NEAR CAMP - EXT/DAY

*A fierce falcon perches on the Khan's gloved hand. He strokes
the masked bird. Zurevno watches with fascination. The Men
have been talking privately.*

FEOFAR KHAN: It is a fine plan, Colonel. You are abso-
   lutely sure the Grand Duke will not suspect you?

ZUREVNO: We have never met, so he doesn't know my face.

We will all be in Russian uniforms. Once we are
inside his stronghold—

FEOFAR KHAN: We will strike!

*The Khan takes off the falcon's mask and lets his bird go. It
flies high, circling in the air above the Men. They watch in
fascination.*

FEOFAR KHAN: If one could fly…such grace….

ZUREVNO: In a sense, your Majesty, you are flying as
    well…across the face of Russia.

FEOFAR KHAN: Yes. I make my way to the sun.

*The Khan shields his eyes from the glare, then his falcon
glides out of the sun's rays and swoops lower to the earth. It
has spotted a rabbit hopping through the tall grass.*

FEOFAR KHAN: All hunters must be careful of their prey.
    What of Czar Alexander?

ZUREVNO: This war has come, and he is not prepared. I
    believe he sits in Moscow, numb and weak.

FEOFAR KHAN: If we conquer Irkutsk…if we bring
    Grand Duke Theodore to his meek little knees
    and take control of the city, his castle and troops,
    armaments—

ZUREVNO: Then, my Lord, the entire East will be at your command.

*The falcon's sharp talons dig into the rabbit's neck. The rabbit bares its teeth, but cannot reach the falcon. Blood spurts as an artery is severed. The rabbit squeals.*

FEOFAR KHAN: Irkutsk is a majestic place. One does not wonder why it is called the Jewel of the East. The mineral oil in the springs is most remarkable. It makes the water glisten, yet one would not expect it to be so deadly. Can you make these springs flow easily?

ZUREVNO: It will be done so that flames are delivered to Theodore's own impotent bed!

*Both Men watch the falcon returning with the rabbit in its talons, dangling down from the sky.*

FEOFAR KHAN: When we succeed, I will appoint you First Governor General of Irkutsk and Supreme Commander of all troops in the region.

ZUREVNO: I am honored.

*The falcon drops the rabbit at the Khan's feet and again perches on his arm.*

FEOFAR KHAN: Thank you for the gift of the chessmen.

It is one of the few Western games I care for. Perhaps we should play together before you leave.

ZUREVNO: I am sure Feofar Khan is a superior gamesman.

FEOFAR KHAN: You flatter me, Colonel, but I assure you,
I do not always win.

ZUREVNO: When have you lost?

FEOFAR KHAN: When I allow my falcon to challenge
me, of course!

*The Men laugh. The Khan strokes his bird tenderly, then
replaces the mask over its face. Zurevno picks up the dead
rabbit.*

*Zurevno and Feofar Khan walk through the grass back
toward camp.*

FEOFAR KHAN: If God were here with us—of course, he is
not—but imagine that he were. What would he
say about our plan, Colonel?

*Zurevno thinks about this seriously.*

ZUREVNO: He would give his blessing to the strong.

*The Khan nods solemnly in agreement.*

## 116. CREEK RUNNING THROUGH CAMP - EXT/DAY

*The Women Prisoners are allowed to bathe. The water is cold. Marfa and Nadia stand near each other. Nadia rinses out her colored scarf to clean her wounded back.*

MARFA: Are you feeling better?

NADIA: Yes. Thank you for helping me.

MARFA: That's a very nice scarf.

NADIA: A man gave it to me…before he was killed.

MARFA: I'm sorry.

NADIA: I didn't know Nicholas long. But I think I loved him.

*The Two Women are sad, but they're comfortable with each other. Marfa whispers quietly, careful not to be heard by the Guards.*

MARFA: I have a son. Michael. I believe he is still alive…but they are looking for him!

NADIA: You are from this region?

MARFA: I live in Omsk.

NADIA: This man who died...I believe his mother was
from Omsk, also.

MARFA: What was his name?

NADIA: Nicholas Korpanoff. He was a horse-trader...and
other things.

MARFA: I don't believe I know his people. Korpanoff? No.
What is his mother's name?

NADIA: I believe he told me it was Marfa.

*The Old Woman looks at her intently.*

MARFA: That is my own name.

NADIA: Is it?

MARFA: Yes. Marfa Strogoff.

NADIA: What a strange coincidence. Well, I'm Nadia
Fedor.

*The Two Women complete their bathing. The Guards steer
all the Captives back to the camp. Nadia notices horses tethered on the other side of the bank.*

## 117. MEN'S CAMP - EXT/DAY

*Mikhail, Jolivet, and Michael crouch quietly by the tiny fire. They whisper so the Guards will not hear.*

MIKHAIL: I'm certain we can do it if we're careful.

JOLIVET: I'm not.

STROGOFF: Will the others fight?

MIKHAIL: Many will join us!

*The Guards order them all to line up. Mikhail walks close to Michael.*

MIKHAIL: Tonight!

*The Men are herded out of their corral to an open place, where Women Prisoners prepare to serve food.*

MIKHAIL: They must be fattening us up for the kill.

*The Men walk in a slow line. Sangarre and the Bohemian watch the Prisoners carefully. Marfa dishes soup from a large kettle. Next to her is Nadia, handing out hard slabs of bread.*

*The Line of Prisoners proceeds gradually. Michael picks up a bowl. When he reaches the kettle, Marfa looks up and is shocked to see him. He is surprised, also. Marfa hesitates with the ladle, but Michael signals her with his eyes.*

*Sangarre notices this recognition between them. She carefully studies Michael, and he seems familiar.*

*Michael moves on—Marfa still watching—and now Nadia suddenly turns and sees him. Her mouth opens, tears fill her eyes. Michael smiles with love and relief. Nadia almost reaches out to touch Michael, but Marfa quickly blocks her arm, pretending to drop the ladle. Michael quickly moves on down the line.*

*None of this is missed by Sangarre. She smiles knowingly.*


## 118. ZUREVNO'S TENT - INT/DAY - MINUTES LATER

*In front of a large mirror, the Colonel admires himself in decorative Tartar dress. Sangarre bursts into the tent, excited and breathless.*

SANGARRE: He's here!

ZUREVNO: Who?

SANGARRE: The Czar's courier! I saw him, Victor!

ZUREVNO: Are you sure?

SANGARRE: Yes! He's with the prisoners! His mother knows him! She could hardly restrain herself!

*Zurevno smiles slyly and tightens the silk sash that holds his new jeweled Asian dagger.*

ZUREVNO: The time has come to talk with the old woman
again. Perhaps the Khan will enjoy this.

*They quickly leave the tent.*

## 119. TARTAR CAMP, CENTRAL PLAZA - EXT/DAY

*The Women Captives are being led into the open area. Marfa
and Nadia walk side-by-side, dazed and confused.*

NADIA: That was your son, wasn't it.

*Marfa nods her head.*

NADIA: He is also the man I love.

*The Women stare at each other with knowledge and fear-
ful recognition.*

*From a different side, all the Men Captives are herded to-
ward the same open area as the Women. Michael makes it a
point to drift away from Jolivet and Mikhail.*

*Guards surround all the Prisoners as they are halted near
the Khan's tent. Feofar Khan, Murga-Ti, Roola, Sangarre,
the Bohemian, and Colonel Zurevno are all there, staring at
the Captives with disdain.*

*Zurevno whispers to Sangarre, and she sends the Bohe-
mian and Peter into the crowd of Women. They grab Marfa
Strogoff.*

*Marfa is brought to the center of the ring. She glares at
Zurevno.*

ZUREVNO: Are you Marfa Strogoff?

MARFA: Yes.

*From deep in the Crowd, Michael looks on desperately.*

ZUREVNO: Have you anything to say to me?

MARFA: No.

*Nadia is horrified. She looks around for Michael but can't find him in all the faces.*

ZUREVNO: Do you admit that your son, Michael Strogoff—courier for the Czar has passed through this territory?

MARFA: I do not know this.

*Feofar Khan's eyes glitter. Murga-Ti nods with pleasure. Zurevno becomes angry.*

ZUREVNO: Listen, old woman! Your son is a prisoner here! You will immediately point him out!

MARFA: No.

*Zurevno is grim. Marfa stands still, but she's very afraid. Michael glares with hatred and grits his teeth, but he stays hidden behind other Men. Nadia is confused. Sangarre's eyes roam the many faces.*

*Zurevno signals to the Guard with the whip. He steps forward. Where once there were thongs in the whip, now there are twisted wires.*

ZUREVNO: I suggest, Old Woman, that you look these men over one more time.

*Marfa stares at all the Captives. Her eyes pass over Michael's without recognition. Michael strains to control himself as he stares at the iron whip.*

MARFA: He is not here. I've said it many times.

*Suddenly, Sangarre's eyes have discovered Michael's. Zurevno looks at her, and she nods.*

ZUREVNO: Do you want to die, Marfa Strogoff? Are you asking me to kill you?

*But she just stands calm and still, her eyes staring through the frustrated Colonel.*

ZUREVNO: So be it!

*Marfa is seized by Two Guards who force her to her knees. They tear the dress from her back, and a saber is placed at her breast to kill her if she moves.*
*The Guard with the whip circles her, then stands close and caresses the long sharp wires.*
*Michael watches in horror, he shivers with great rage and despair. Then he starts slowly through the Crowd.*

*Zurevno and Sangarre see him coming. The Prisoners make way. But the Guard with the whip doesn't notice—he raises his weapon—*

*Michael suddenly runs and leaps high in the air, coming down on the Guard with the whip so strong he knocks him over. Michael slams his fist into his face, then grabs the whip away.*

*Guards immediately surround Michael. The Khan smiles.*

FEOFAR KHAN: Wonderful!

*Zurevno gloats with satisfaction as Michael lifts his Mother from the ground. They embrace.*

STROGOFF: I love you, Mother.

*Nadia looks on with tears in her eyes. Zurevno walks forward and waves the Guards away.*

ZUREVNO: Michael Strogoff!

*He stares at Michael hard, remembering him.*

ZUREVNO: We have met, haven't we? You're the coward from the station!

*Zurevno smirks but Michael glares at him and suddenly raises the whip. He slashes Zurevno's face. The Colonel falls bleeding to the ground. Guards jump Michael and beat him in the dirt.*

*Marfa screams. Nadia runs to her. In the back of the Crowd,*

*Jolivet and Mikhail slowly drift from Man to Man, whispering.*

*Zurevno stands, blood flowing from his forehead. The Khan is now less amused, but he still watches intently.*

ZUREVNO: Search him!

*The Guards tear open Michael's clothes. The dispatch pouch falls out. Zurevno picks it up and opens it. He smiles at the Imperial wax seal.*

*Nadia is horrified. Marfa seems to be in shock. Jolivet and Mikhail continue to drift to the periphery of the Crowd. Sangarre is ecstatic by the turn of events.*

*Blood from Zurevno's face drips onto the parchment as he reads the Czar's message to the Grand Duke. The Khan stares at Michael grimly.*

FEOFAR KHAN: A Russian spy!

MURGA-TI: He must be punished!

FEOFAR KHAN: What did you hope to see here, Russian spy?

*Michael doesn't answer. The Guards bend his arms back, causing him great pain.*

FEOFAR KHAN: Answer! What do you see?

STROGOFF: Madness and evil!

*The Khan smiles maliciously.*

FEOFAR KHAN: Take a good long look, then…while you
    still can.

*The Khan signals to Murga-Ti, who approaches Zurevno
and whispers. The Colonel smiles, then draws his dagger, which
Murga-Ti takes. The Tartar sticks the blade into a fire of
coals near Roola.*

*Michael struggles with the Guards, but they hold him firmly.
The Khan watches with delight. The plaza is tense with ex-
pectation.*

*Murga-Ti removes the dagger from the coals. The blade is
white-hot. Roola says a prayer over it. Murga-Ti hands the
dagger back to Zurevno.*

*Marfa screams in anguish. Guards hold her. Nadia struggles
with them, then breaks through the circle and runs toward
Zurevno. He's amused as Other Guards knock Nadia to the
ground before she can reach him.*

*Michael watches all this sadly. Zurevno stands before him,
the hot blade in one hand, the bloody dispatch in the other.*

ZUREVNO: So, courier! You were to warn the Grand Duke
    about me!

STROGOFF: Zurevno, you are a traitor and a coward.

ZUREVNO: Am I?

*The Colonel can hardly control his rage. He steps closer
with the knife. Michael watches the glowing blade.*

ZUREVNO: Perhaps you would like to try fighting me
again. Yes?

*Zurevno signals for the Guards to release Michael—but
before they let go—as Michael's face is slightly turned—
Zurevno slashes with the knife across Michael's eyes.*

*Michael groans in pain. Blood pours from his face and fills
the left eye socket. He falls to the ground.*

*Marfa screams with anguish, and suddenly a pain sears
through her chest. She slumps to the ground. Staring at her
Son, she breathes her last. Nadia looks in horror at Michael,
then at Marfa. She cries in agony.*

*Zurevno gloats. He stoops down near Michael and picks at
the pool of blood with his dagger point. Then he finds it—the
eye! He gently picks it up, carries it in the palm of his hand to
the Khan. The Khan nods with approval, then Roola takes it
and places it in the fire.*

*Suddenly there is chaos. The Prisoners yell viciously! There
is gunfire! Guards are knocked from their horses. Mikhail
stabs several Tartars. Jolivet grabs a torch and throws it into a
tent. The Prisoners revolt! More guns blaze, spears are turned
inward at the Tartars. Guards are jumped, their horses taken.
More torches are thrown. Mikhail rides close to the Khan's
tent and slings fire into it. Smoke billows. Pandemonium everywhere. Zurevno ducks as an arrow passes over him. The
Prisoners frighten the Tartars with their savagery and rage,
and as a Mass they attack and fight to the death.*

*Smoke completely covers the central plaza. Nadia is quickly
beside Michael. She holds him, his blood spilling over her.
Under the cover of smoke, she is able to help lift him off the
ground. They run for their lives!*

## 120. THE CREEK - EXT/DAY

*They struggle across the bank. She pulls Michael down into the water. She catches her breath. Michael is stunned, confused, in great shock and pain. Tartars ride along the shore...but when they pass, Nadia leads Michael across the creek. Smoke still covers the terrain.*

*Horses are tethered on the other side. They're spooked by the noise and fire. Nadia unties a stallion, tries to get Michael to climb on, but he falls.*

NADIA: You have to help me! We can get away! Please—

*Michael gathers clarity and lifts himself to the stallion's flank. Nadia holds him, steadies the horse, then pushes as Michael hefts himself onto the stallion's back. Nadia quickly climbs up in front of him, forces his arms around her waist so he'll hold on—and they ride.*

## 121. AFTERWARD - THE TARTAR CAMP.

*Bodies and blood cover the ground. Most of the Prisoners have been killed, but many Tartars are also dead. Zurevno wanders the smoky battlefield...searching. He grabs corpses up by the hair to stare at their faces. He raises his sword...but he can't find the courier he's so desperate to kill.*

෨

## 122. A BURNED-OUT HUT IN THE FOREST - INT/NIGHT

*Snow is falling. Michael huddles dazed before a low fire. Nadia gathers bark and leaves, mixes it with mud, then grinds it all with a stone.*

JOLIVET'S NARRATION [*voice-over*]: "It was a miracle the lovers had been able to escape...that any of us had. But I'm convinced that although the Fates are malicious and cruel, sometimes they surprise us mortals with their strange sense of justice... especially if we have suffered enough for them... performed our grim duty as their pawns..."

*Nadia applies the mixture to Michael's ruined eye-wound. She takes her colored scarf and wraps it tightly around his face.*

NADIA: This poultice will help. My father taught me how to do it.

*Michael's surviving eye is closed, the cut across the brow very painful. But he slowly opens it and stares into the fire. A faint haze emerges to him.*

NADIA: Can you see anything at all, Michael?

STROGOFF: I'm not sure.

*Nadia holds him tightly in her arms.*

NADIA: I will take care of you.

STROGOFF: Nadia, we must keep moving. I must get to
Irkutsk…warn the Grand Duke.

NADIA: I know, my love. You must trust me.


## 123. THE FOREST - EXT/DAY

MONTAGE: *The snow is deep, covering the trees and the
ground. They trudge slowly on horseback. Michael's single eye
roams: all he sees is hazy whiteness. They are cold and tired.
Nadia watches him with great worry. The snow thickens. They
dismount to drink the snow. Nadia finds some roots they chew
on and feeds some to the horse. It grows weak, digging its nose
into the snow searching for food. Michael struggles to keep his
eye open, to find some sharpness in the constant blur.*

*They reach a trail, more snow falls. They keep moving
against the wind.*

*At times Nadia leads the weakened horse, but keeps Michael
in the saddle. The wind picks up. Eventually, the horse falls
in a snow bank. Michael is thrown free. The poor animal
will not get up. They leave it and continue trudging along
down the trail.*

## 123a. LATER

*Michael is so weak that Nadia lifts him onto her back. They struggle up a hill, but then she can carry him no longer. They fall.*

NADIA: We must keep going, love. Or we'll freeze.

*She tries to help him walk, but he just sits.*

STROGOFF: I hear something.

NADIA: It is just the wind.

STROGOFF: No. There!

*Nadia has heard it, too. A distant sound like a horse and wagon.*

STROGOFF: We must be very careful.

*They stand close to a huge tree where branches of snow hide them. They wait quietly.*
*In the distance, coming down the trail, there's a sled! And two horses! Nadia stares at it, but Michael can only make out a blurry motion.*

STROGOFF: How many people?

NADIA: Only a driver.

*The sled comes closer.*

NADIA: A strange man...he seems to be a hunchback....

*Michael suddenly smiles, then breaks away from her and runs.*

STROGOFF: We must stop him, Nadia! I think I know this man!

*Nadia runs after him in the snow. Michael falls and she picks him up. They make it to the middle of the trail. Michael waves his arms.*
*From his sled, Serko sees them. He is delighted and surprised. He reins the sled to a halt.*

STROGOFF: Serko! Is that you?

*The Hunchback nods enthusiastically, but he suddenly frowns when he sees how hurt Michael is. He embraces Michael.*
*Nadia smiles at the Men. She looks in the sled and sees furs, blankets, provisions.*

STROGOFF: Will you help us, Serko? Things have gone very bad. We must get to Irkutsk!

*Serko energetically nods his head. There are tears in his eyes. He happily helps Michael onto the sled, then Nadia.*
*Michael sees: a hulking blur when he looks at Serko.*

STROGOFF: Is this the old sled you had in your hut?

*Serko nods.*

STROGOFF: You're a wonder!

*Serko smiles again, then he whips the reins and the horses begin to gallop. The sled jerks and speeds down the trail.*


## 124. SOME FIELDS - EXT/DAY

*In the sled, Nadia wraps Michael with a blanket. Serko looks back at her while he drives.*

NADIA: I'm Nadia Fedor.

*Serko nods pleasantly, then points to a basket, indicating she should open it. She finds fruit, nuts, bread, cheese, wine. Nadia smiles with grateful pleasure. She breaks off pieces of food, hands some to both Men. She helps Michael drink some wine, it spills down his chin. She whispers quietly.*

NADIA: Was he unable to speak at birth?

STROGOFF: The Tartars cut out his tongue.

*Nadia remains solemn as the sled races across the land.*

## 125. CLEARING IN A FOREST - EXT/NIGHT

*They eat before a small campfire. Michael drinks rum excessively. The horses graze near the sled.*

NADIA: Have you seen much hardship on the road, Serko?

*The Hunchback nods solemnly.*

NADIA: These are such difficult times.

*Michael is getting drunk.*

STROGOFF: They killed my mother…they beat Nadia and raped her…they've taken my eye and your tongue, Serko….

*Nadia reaches for the bottle to take it away, but Michael holds it tight.*

STROGOFF: Vengeance is the only thing that will satisfy me now!

*He stares into the fire, his wide eye reflecting light: The hazy flames dance, then become clear, then hazy again. He blinks hard: clarity again returns and it stays!*
*Michael smiles to himself and drinks more.*

STROGOFF: The Angara River is near. I can smell it! Our last obstacle before Irkutsk!

*Serko watches Michael closely, then he waves to the sled. He claps his hands loudly for attention, but nobody understands what he's doing. So he pulls out two long poles that have been strapped to the side. He slips them together, fastened by a hinge. Then he sticks the cross in the center of the sled into a wedged nook, newly carved-out.*

*Nadia and Michael watch in fascination.*

*Serko unwraps a large white cloth. He holds it tight in the wind then fastens it to the cross. It's the Russian flag! Nadia finally understands.*

NADIA: A boat! Michael, he's made a boat!

*Michael sees the white flag sharply, the emblem of the Two-Headed Eagle waving in the wind.*

STROGOFF: You're a genius, Serko! A mad, glorious genius!

*The Hunchback smiles shyly at their appreciation. Then he rummages through the provisions, brings out some objects, and places them in Michael's lap.*

*Two pistols and two large Siberian hunting knives. Michael handles them lovingly. Nadia watches, worried. Michael keeps drinking. Soon he settles back asleep. Then Nadia carefully takes the weapons from him and wraps them in a blanket where they'll be safe.*

## 126. THE CAMPSITE - EXT/DAWN

*The smoldering fire catches snowflakes. Nadia, Michael, and Serko sleep quietly. The flag atop the sled is still. Two dark Tartar eyes watch through the grass—*

*Suddenly, Three Tartars on horseback crash through the camp, swinging their long clubs. They yell drunkenly. Serko is the first to rise, and he's smashed in the head by a club. Then a lance is thrown which runs him through, sticking him to a tree. Nadia screams, then another club fells her.*

*Michael is up and looking for the Attackers: but it's a haze to him. He scrambles for his weapons, but can't find them. A rope is thrown over him, and the drunken Tartars laugh as he reels and stumbles. Then a Rider passes and strikes Michael with the long club as well.*

*The Tartars dismount. They laugh at the Hunchback dead at the tree. A Tartar lifts Nadia by the hair, but she's unconscious. He tries to pour liquor in her mouth, but it dribbles out.*

*Michael is tied upright to a horse, and the animal trots back and forth around the campsite. The Tartars laugh uproariously. They swish by in Michael's vision, but he's able to control the horse with his thighs. He works the ropes at his wrists.*

*The Tartar near Nadia keeps staring, then slowly climbs on top of her.*

*The other Two Tartars drink and laugh. One of them fires an arrow at Michael but misses. The other smirks at his Friend on top of Nadia, but the Molester becomes still.*

*The Tartar walks over, rolls his Friend off the Woman. There's a knife in the Man's stomach! Nadia rolls away, a pistol in her hand. She shoots the Tartar in the face.*

*The last Tartar yells in anger. He races toward Nadia with a lance—but Michael has loosened his bonds enough to steer the horse. He tramples the Tartar to death!*

## 127. LATER

*Michael has finished burying Serko. Nadia is in tears. She picks a holly branch and places it on the grave.*

STROGOFF: He was a…our guardian angel. The Gods sent him to us, now they have reclaimed him. He will find his new voice in paradise.

NADIA: Why don't the good people survive, Michael? Why are we all being turned into killers?

*Michael stares at the dead Tartars angrily. In a rage he picks up a sword and slashes them, over and over again.*

༄

## 128. THE ANGARA RIVER - EXT/DAY

*Ice floes dot the raging waters. Nadia and Michael ride on shore in the sled. The wind catches the flag/sail. They quickly set the horses free and shove the sled into the current. Then they jump, riding the water.*

*The current is very unsteady, but when they stand carefully and balance, the sled/boat floats smoother. With the long Tartar lances and clubs, they maneuver among the ice flows.*

*The wind blows Nadia's hair wildly. Michael is able to finally focus his eye for longer periods. He sees: winter hawks circling above until the sky's glare makes him wince in pain.*

*They make good time. The river is long.*


## 129. MONTAGE:

*Time passes. The sun alters from morning to late afternoon. The boat/sled is tiny in the expanse of the great river. The ice blocks grow larger and more difficult to navigate through. Nadia and Michael struggle with the poles, but their work is steady.*

*A fierce howling is heard. On the bank is a pack of wolves! Some of them are rabid, with foam dripping from their mouths. One wolf leaps onto an ice block, another follows. They head toward the boat/sled.*

*Nadia aims the pistol and fires. A wolf is hit and falls into the river. Michael stands ready with his lance and sword, Nadia points the other gun. But the wolves now just stare and are still. They allow the boat/sled to pass.*


## 130. DUSK

*They see a distant glow on the far horizon. To Michael: the sky is hazy, but he knows what the light means.*

NADIA: It's Irkutsk.

*They round a bend and the fortress-city stands majestically in silhouette against the sky.*

*Now the ice blocks are so thick it's impossible to maneuver the small craft. The ice on the current bunches up, wedging against the sled/boat. The pressure is so great the wood starts to crack.*

*They climb off onto an ice block. Suddenly the wood splinters! They've made it clear just in time. The boat/sled sinks into the river.*

*Slowly, carefully, Nadia leads Michael across the slippery ice. They both fall, Nadia slipping into the water. Michael pulls her back. An oily substance is on her clothes, and on Michael's sleeve, also.*

STROGOFF: What is this?

*He tries to wipe it off.*

NADIA: It's an oil, called naphtha. Comes from the springs in the hills.

*They notice that the mineral oil is swirling in the current.*

NADIA: This is very dangerous.

STROGOFF: Why?

NADIA: Because I've seen this oil burn. My father has experimented with it. Even this river could catch on fire. There must be a leak in the reservoir.

*Michael strains to see high into the hills. Irkutsk is so close that Nadia can reach out her hand and pretend the huge fortress and walls are being touched.*

NADIA: What a beautiful city!

*They continue carefully walking from ice block to ice block in the river. Suddenly they see tiny streaks of light in the sky near Irkutsk, a stream of flickering that arcs from one side of the river to the other, ending near the distant fortress.*

NADIA: Michael, I want to believe in shooting stars. But
       I'm sure those were flaming arrows from the other
       bank!

STROGOFF: We had better hurry, Nadia.

*But the ice blocks are difficult, and the shore is a distance away.*

☙

## 131. THE RESERVOIR, IN THE HILLS - EXT/DUSK - AT THIS SAME TIME

*Russian Guards lay dead in the snow. Zurevno, in Russian uniform, watches as Peter and the Bohemian, also uniformed, widen the hole in the huge clay wall. A stream of oil continues down the hill toward the river below.*
*Sangarre and Old Louis, in Tartar dress, keep watch.*

ZUREVNO: The current will carry the naphtha oil directly
        to the castle. Then, at the correct moment, I will
        ignite the stream.

SANGARRE: What if they see you...or you are late.

ZUREVNO: Then I'm sure one of the Khan's arrows will soon do the job. But I want to be more precise. It is the west wall that must go up in flames.

SANGARRE: When will you secure the Bolchia gate?

ZUREVNO: Hopefully, within the hour. When you see the flames at the west wall, you will know we're at the gate.

*Sangarre stares at the Colonel with affection. He mounts his horse, she hers. They move close and kiss.*

SANGARRE: I am with you always, Victor.

ZUREVNO: You will be my queen.

## 132. IRKUTSK, THE FORTRESS-CITY - EXT/DUSK

*From the ramparts, General Yuragon studies the Tartar Army across the river. Through his telescope: the Hordes are strong in number and camped in the forest. Their camp fires string out along the fields.*

*Suddenly, more flaming arrows are shot, but most of them fizzle at the foot of the stone wall or die in the river. The ice moves with the current. He sees many Tartars try to cross over, and he laughs when they have to turn back.*

*He signals to his Lieutenant. A line of Soldiers aim their rifles. He signals and the guns fire. Through the scope: Yuragon sees many Tartars fall dead.*

GENERAL YURAGON: Good work, men! Choose your
targets. We've got to make the bullets last.

*Suddenly the night is filled with other shots, and several
Soldiers are hit. Tartar bullets ricochet on the stone.*


## 133. THE TARTAR CAMP - EXT/DUSK

*The Khan also watches through a telescope: and he smiles at
the Russian dead. Murga-Ti prepares a column of archers.
They fire—a hundred arrows of flame streaking high across
the river!*


## 134. IRKUTSK - EXT/DUSK

*This time the arrows reach the ramparts. One strikes a Sol-
dier in the chest, igniting him. Other arrows land on sheds or
walls, and the fires must be put out quickly.*
  *General Yuragon watches the sun sink into the water.*

GENERAL YURAGON: Please God, give us darkness.


## 135. THE FOREST, NEAR THE BOLCHIA GATE
## EXT/NIGHT

*All on horseback, Zurevno, Peter, and the Bohemian stare at
the huge wall. Sangarre and Old Louis have stopped a good
distance apart.*

ZUREVNO: The Bolchia gate! Achilles heel of this fortress!

*He looks back to Sangarre and Old Louis, who draw their guns.*

ZUREVNO: Are you ready?

SANGARRE: Yes.

ZUREVNO: Play your parts well.

*Sangarre and Old Louis fire their guns. Zurevno, Peter, and the Bohemian race out of the trees, screaming. Sangarre and Louis fire again, yelling after them.*
*The Men ride toward the gate as if being chased. From high on the ramparts, the Russian Soldiers aim their rifles. Zurevno yells at them in panic.*

ZUREVNO: Open the gate for us!


## 136. ON THE RAMPARTS - EXT/NIGHT

*The Guard Captain stares down at the "Russians".*

GUARD CAPTAIN: Who's there? Are you Russian?

ZUREVNO: Please! Let us in! Tartars are behind us!

*Sangarre and Old Louis can be seen in Tartar dress riding in the trees.*

ZUREVNO: I am the Czar's courier! With a message for
the Grand Duke!

*Zurevno holds up the dispatch, and from his vantage point
it seems official to the Guard Captain. He signals more Soldiers to guard the wall and aim their weapons. Other Soldiers man the huge cauldrons of hot oil and burning coals.*

GUARD CAPTAIN: Open the gate, but only enough for a
horse to get through.


## 137. THE CLEARING - EXT/NIGHT

*Zurevno and his men see the iron gate squeak open just a
little bit, but it's enough. They ride through as fast as they
can.*


## 138. THE COURTYARD - EXT/NIGHT

*Rifles and crossbows are trained on the Men. Zurevno smiles
at the Guard Captain.*

ZUREVNO: We thought the damn savages would get us
this time! Bless you all!

*The Soldiers lower their weapons at Zurevno's friendli-
ness. Peter and the Bohemian smile also. They dismount.*

GUARD CAPTAIN: Where are you coming from?

ZUREVNO: Moscow. We've ridden thousands of miles to deliver this dispatch to Grand Duke Theodore. I must see him immediately, Captain.

*The Guard Captain stares again at the paper—at the Imperial seal pressed in red wax.*

GUARD CAPTAIN: I'll take you there myself. Your men will remain here!

ZUREVNO: Yes, sir.

*Zurevno makes a show of straightening his uniform, then he follows the Guard Captain into the castle.*

## 139. THE GRAND DUKE'S CHAMBERS - INT/NIGHT

*Theodore looks sadly out his window at the fires the Soldiers and Townspeople are putting out. The Wounded are being carried away. Across the river, the fires from the Tartar camp glisten. The Grand Duke's face is solemn.*

*In a gilded cage near the window, a golden nightingale flutters in fear. Theodore reaches in and takes the bird in his hands to calm it. On a wall is a portrait of Czar Alexander and Czarina Catherine. The resemblance between the Two Brothers is uncanny. They are very nearly twins.*

*General Yuragon stands thoughtfully near the fireplace. His face is grimy with dirt and blood.*

GRAND DUKE: Why can't we attack in force?

GENERAL YURAGON: They are too far away, Sire. The river protects them…and us, I might add. Also, we're not sure how many are out there.

GRAND DUKE: What have the scouts reported?

GENERAL YURAGON: I'm afraid no scouts have returned.

GRAND DUKE: Damn!

GENERAL YURAGON: The river is keeping the Tartars at bay. As long as the ice keeps in motion, some men can cross, but not their entire army.

GRAND DUKE: General Yuragon, do you think we can hold the siege until reinforcements arrive?

*The General is thoughtful. Both Men fear the worst.*

GENERAL YURAGON: I hope so, Sire.

GRAND DUKE: Hope. Exactly what we need.

GENERAL YURAGON: We command seasoned troops, Sire. The best fighters in the world. The question is one of numbers. We should have been more alert, more aware of the possibility of this threat.

GRAND DUKE: Our task has always been to defend this

territory. Not to wage campaigns on the border every time we hear rumors of a raid or skirmish!

GENERAL YURAGON: Perhaps. But if we had posted more troops in the interior, we could have halted this build-up before it got out of hand.

GRAND DUKE: That is pure speculation, General!

*The Men are tense and angry. The situation is unbearable. Theodore pours a chalice of wine and hands it to Yuragon.*

GENERAL YURAGON: Theodore, the refugees who came in this afternoon reported Russian troops in Tobsk. I believe there is help coming…we just can't be sure when.

GRAND DUKE: My brother would never forsake us.

*He places the golden nightingale back in the cage. It is calmer.*
*There's a knock on the door.*

GRAND DUKE: Enter!

*Major Alekim comes in, bows then salutes.*

MAJOR ALEKIM: Sire, the man insists. He will not leave the palace. There is no threat of violence, but with eight Siberians…arresting them all would cause turmoil we do not need.

GRAND DUKE: Damn that old man!

GENERAL YURAGON: Who is this?

GRAND DUKE: That exile from Moscow. Fedor. He has
          petitioned me repeatedly, demanding that I let
          him volunteer. He has some sort of invention the
          army needs…he says!

GENERAL YURAGON: We can use every fighter we can
          get, Sire.

GRAND DUKE: He is a crank! Alexander exiled him for
          his strange medical practices…his membership
          in some perverse secret society….

GENERAL YURAGON: I know of the "Illuminati". But
          in my experience they are not all bad fellows.

GRAND DUKE: I have no desire to patronize one of my
          brother's outcasts!

*The room is tense. Major Alekim clears his throat.*

GRAND DUKE: Do you have something to say, Major?

MAJOR ALEKIM: Well, Sire…it's my opinion…if you
          don't mind me saying it…these Siberians are fierce
          fighters. And this old man commands an entire
          band of them!

*The Grand Duke thinks this over.*

GENERAL YURAGON: We are very short-handed, Theodore.

GRAND DUKE: All right, gentlemen! I will talk to the man!

*The Major ushers in Wassili Fedor. The Old Man's hair is long and white. He wears huntsman leathers and a jewel around his neck. A pouch hangs from his shoulder. He bows.*

FEDOR: Sire! I implore you! My men and I are at your service in this time of trouble.

GRAND DUKE: My brother, Czar Alexander, holds you in disfavor, sir. He says that as a physician you incorporate unholy practices.

FEDOR: I heal the sick and wounded. My methods work to this effect. Your brother was angered...by other things. Things he chose to remain ignorant of.

GRAND DUKE: You are an alchemist? A spell-maker?

FEDOR: Superstition!

GRAND DUKE: You have a friend in General Yuragon. And in Major Alekim, also. They believe you and your band can be of use.

FEDOR: My men are true fighters. Excellent marksmen!

*Theodore nods and defers to General Yuragon. He goes back to the window to stare down at his Subjects. Wagons are being upturned in the square so People can use them as shields from the arrows.*

GENERAL YURAGON: We are short-handed along the western wall near the Bolchia gate. Do you know the place?

FEDOR: Yes. The enemy would have to come by way of the forest to attack. But the gate is so small. Only foot-soldiers could ever pass through, and not many of those at one time.

GENERAL YURAGON: You obviously know something about war, Mr. Fedor. Position your men there.

FEDOR: Yes, sir.

*Wassili Fedor turns to leave, but the Grand Duke will not look at him. He's too intent at the window. So the Old Man takes a bottle from his pouch.*

FEDOR: Gentlemen, I have something here that could be of great help to us.

*The Grand Duke finally turns and frowns.*

GRAND DUKE: What is this foolishness? You try my patience, old man.

FEDOR: May I demonstrate?

*They watch, astonished by his boldness. Fedor goes to the fireplace. He removes a shield from the wall, then lays it down on the stones. He uncorks the small bottle and pours the liquid onto the shield.*

*It smokes and burns through. The Men are fascinated.*

MAJOR ALEKIM: The devil's potion!

FEDOR: I call it "acyde". If this special mixture is rained down on the Tartars, it will penetrate their shields and be more effective than oil or hot coals.

GENERAL YURAGON: Remarkable!

FEDOR: Imagine what my acyde would do to human flesh.

GRAND DUKE: This is extraordinary, Fedor. I commend you…and apologize for my skepticism. But I also feel this is a very evil weapon!

*The Old Man is solemn. He places the bottle on Theodore's desk.*

FEDOR: Yes. Evil. I agree. Yet only these Tartars deserve it, since they would do much worse to all of us if Irkutsk fell into their hands!

*Suddenly a loud noise shatters the discussion, the chambers shake. Dust falls. Then another retort stuns the Men.*

GENERAL YURAGON: This is what we feared! The Khan
    has a cannon! Major Alekim!

*The Major runs from the chambers. Looking down from
the window, the General and Grand Duke watch the Russian cannons shift into position. Major Alekim gives the order, and they fire.*


## 140. THE TARTAR CAMP - EXT/NIGHT

*One cannon ball flies far wide of the Tartars. Murga-Ti and
the Khan laugh when it hits the nearby forest, felling trees. As
the Warriors load their own cannon, the other Russian ball
sails closer—landing in the Tartar corral, killing many horses.*

*The Khan is grim. Murga-Ti commands the Warriors to
aim lower, and the cannon is fired.*


## 141. THE FORTRESS - EXT/NIGHT

*The Tartar shell lands in the river far from the wall. The
Russian Artillerymen are sprayed with water that rises to the
ramparts. They fire another round.*


## 142. TARTAR CAMP - EXT/NIGHT

*This shell lands near the Tartar tents, demolishing several
and causing fires. Tartar Warriors run to put out the flames,
hurrying back and forth from the river with casks and buck-
ets.*

*The Khan is enraged. Roola, standing near, prays to the huge gun. Murga-Ti orders water poured on the muzzle, where it's so hot it smokes.*

FEOFAR KHAN: Fire at them again! Immediately!

MURGA-TI: We must wait. The cannon is too hot!

*The Khan is enraged and anxious. He storms over to the cannon, an ancient hard clay model shaped like a dragon's mouth. He sees the tiny crack in the muzzle but waves it away.*

FEOFAR KHAN: It will last the battle. My father defeated the Turks with it—

MURGA-TI: Excellency—

FEOFAR KHAN: Shoot!

*The Warriors fearfully load it up, then fire. The cannon blasts apart. Lead and clay spews through the air, wounding several Tartars. Roola lays dead with her head split open.*

## 143. GRAND DUKE'S CHAMBERS - INT/NIGHT

*The Men are tense in the stillness. Then they relax. Suddenly there's a knock on the door. A Guard enters, obviously one of Theodore's Aides. He walks confidently to the Grand Duke and whispers to him, then exits.*

GRAND DUKE: I knew Alexander would send someone
to me!

GENERAL YURAGON: What is it?

GRAND DUKE: A courier from Moscow! He's in the castle!

*Wassili Fedor becomes thoughtful. Then he bows and exits.*

## 144. CORRIDOR - INT/NIGHT - MOMENTS LATER

*The Old Man stops as he sees Zurevno led by the Guard Captain. They pass, heading toward the Grand Duke's chambers. When Fedor calls out, they stop.*

FEDOR: Sir! Are you the man from Moscow?

ZUREVNO: I am.

FEDOR: Could I ask you a question, please?

ZUREVNO: I must see the Grand Duke.

FEDOR: Yes. But…you have traveled across the territory,
haven't you? By coach? By boat, perhaps?

*It is obvious that Fedor is concerned about something.*

*Zurevno is suspicious, but he tries to be cordial under the watchful eye of the Guard Captain.*

ZUREVNO: My journey took several modes of transportation, of course.

FEDOR: My daughter, Nadia Fedor…a young woman. In your travels did you ever see such a person, or hear of her?

ZUREVNO: Nadia Fedor? No.

FEDOR: She left Moscow weeks ago, at about the same time you must have. I believe she probably took a similar route.

ZUREVNO: No, I'm sorry. There were many incidents, many people. Chaos everywhere.

*Fedor is saddened by this news. Zurevno bows to him and walks on down the long winding corridor.*

## 145. ON THE BATTLEMENTS - EXT/NIGHT

*Fedor supervises the mixing of his acyde into cauldrons. His Siberians take stations near the Bolchia gate. Peter and the Bohemian are there, trying to appear casual but alert.*

## 146. IN THE TREES - EXT/NIGHT

*Sangarre and Old Louis watch the fortress. Gradually a large number of Tartars join them. They have silently crossed the river. All Warriors watch the battlements. Sangarre sees the Bohemian in a high corner, looking toward her.*

## 147. IN THE RIVER - EXT/NIGHT

*Michael and Nadia still make their way along the ice. Once they try to cross to shore, but there is so much mud and slush they are forced to stay on the ice blocks. Michael slips in the dark, falling on his face. He groans in pain. Nadia helps him up to see his eye-wound is bleeding again. But they now reach a solid portion of ice and can walk a bit steadier. They breathe heavily, weak with frustration. But they are near the fortress.*

## 148. GRAND DUKE'S CHAMBERS - INT/NIGHT

*The Guard Captain enters with Zurevno, who bows deeply to Theodore. He salutes General Yuragon.*

GRAND DUKE: You are the courier?

ZUREVNO: Yes, Sire. I bring word to you from your brother, the gracious Czar.

*Theodore smiles with delight. Zurevno hands him the dispatch.*

GENERAL YURAGON: Your name, soldier?

ZUREVNO: Lieutenant Michael Strogoff!

*Theodore stares at the parchment, the torn paper, the ripped wax seal.*

GRAND DUKE: This has been opened!

ZUREVNO: Please forgive me, Sire. It was unavoidable. I was forced to fold it into little bits to better hide it from the enemy.

GRAND DUKE: Have you read this dispatch, Strogoff?

ZUREVNO: On your brother's orders…in case the paper was lost or destroyed.

GENERAL YURAGON: You look like you've gone through much hardship, Lieutenant. That's a recent wound.

*The General indicates Zurevno's gash from the whip. Zurevno lightly touches the scar in a dramatic, solemn way.*

ZUREVNO: I was taken prisoner by the Tartars near Omsk. Luckily I was able to escape before they discovered who I was. The two men I brought with me are the sole survivors of Captain Ravski's patrol.

GENERAL YURAGON: You are to be commended. Your men, also.

*The Grand Duke is absorbed in the dispatch.*

GRAND DUKE: But tell us what you know about this
        Colonel Zurevno.

ZUREVNO: I know that he is the vilest traitor!

*They're impressed by Zurevno's "passion".*
*Theodore hands the dispatch to Yuragon, who reads it*
*quickly.*

GENERAL YURAGON: Have you ever seen this Zurevno?
        Can you describe him to us?

ZUREVNO: He's a younger man, especially for being a
        colonel, in my opinion. But that alone should
        tell you how crafty he is. He's soft-spoken, a strong
        build. His hair is blond but he may have changed
        it in disguise. Yet the one thing he cannot alter is
        that he has only one eye!

GENERAL YURAGON: A one-eyed man! We will watch
        for him!

GRAND DUKE: You are a brave soldier, Strogoff, to have
        gotten through the Tartar lines. How many war-
        riors would you estimate there are?

*Zurevno thinks about this and replies slyly.*

ZUREVNO: I would say the Khan has nearly 50,000 men.

*The Grand Duke and General both go pale at this exaggeration.*

GENERAL YURAGON: Can we expect reinforcements from the west?

ZUREVNO: I'm sorry, sir. I don't believe so. After Captain Ravski's massacre—

GRAND DUKE: But we've received reports from refugees! Russian troops have been sighted. Perhaps General Nerensky's command?

ZUREVNO: I don't know how that's possible, Sire. I've been all over the territory. There is no one.

*The Grand Duke's face is sad and grim.*

GRAND DUKE: Then it is God's will that we stand alone. But we must never allow Irkutsk to be taken, even if a million troops are sent against us!

*The General nods in agreement. So does Zurevno.*


## 149. A GUEST ROOM - INT/NIGHT

*A Pretty Maid shows Zurevno the way to his quarters. She opens the door for him.*

ZUREVNO: And what is your name?

MAID: I'm Maria, Lieutenant Strogoff.

*He smiles and lightly touches her hair, but she moves back, unable to take her eyes from the long gash across his face. She hurries back down the hall. Zurevno sees himself in the mirror, tries to laugh his pain away, but can't.*

*At the large window he can see across to the Tartar camp. All is quiet. There is a telescope near his bed. He adjusts it and stares down at the river: tracing how it connects with the castle's moat.*

*He can make out: oil in the torchlight from the battlements. Zurevno smiles to himself, then goes to his door. The corridor is quiet, so he sneaks out. He grabs a lighted torch from the wall and makes his way in silence.*

## 150. THE BOLCHIA GATE - EXT/NIGHT

*Peter and the Bohemian have passed a bottle of rum to the Russian Guards. They all laugh in the fighting's lull, no longer cautious or too worried. Zurevno appears in the shadows of a wall. Bohemian sees him, nods to Peter. They both jump the Two Guards and cut their throats. The Bodies are thrown silently off the wall into the bordering moat.*

*The moat circles around to the river. Zurevno walks along the battlements with the torch.*

*From the western corner, Wassili Fedor sees the torch in motion. He walks toward it casually, seeing the face of "the Courier" illuminated. Suddenly the torch is thrown over the wall—Zurevno disappears in the momentary darkness—and in his place a sheet of flames rises up the wall from below.*

*Fedor signals for some of his Siberians to follow him. They run along the wall and stare in horror at the river and moat on fire. In the incredible light, Fedor sees that the Bolchia gate is not guarded. No Soldiers are on the wall. Down below are Peter and the Bohemian. They have opened the gate. The Bodies of Two Guards float in the fiery moat.*

*Fedor aims his crossbow and shoots the Bohemian through the throat. Peter signals to Sangarre and the Tartars on the other side, then turns to see his dead companion. A Siberian throws a lance skewering Peter's body between wall and gate.*

*The Tartars and Deserters are coming out of the forest, riding wildly toward the small gate opening. Only Fedor and the Siberians see them, because the other Russian Soldiers are busy trying to put out the fires at the west wall.*

*Several Siberians climb down to try to shut the gate, but it's too late. One Man struggles to remove Peter's Body and is shot by Old Louis. Another Man is trampled by Sangarre's horse when she leaps high over both Bodies into the court-yard. For a moment all are stunned by the Woman's remarkable feat. The Tartar Warriors behind her yell encouragement.*

*Unseen by the Invaders, Fedor tilts the cauldrons from his place on the wall. When the horses race through the gate— the Tartars yelling in apparent victory—the oil/acyde mixture rains down on them from above. Sangarre is one of the first to be burned, in her face. She screams in torment and falls from her horse. Old Louis watches, then aims his pistol at Fedor. Acyde falls on his arm, and his gun falls from his hand.*

*Most of the Tartars writhe in agony from the burning, and fall from their horses. Some are crushed beneath the hooves of their tormented animals. Major Alekim and his Riflemen*

*run along the ramparts, take aim, and shoot the remaining
Invaders without mercy.*

## 151. ON THE RIVER - EXT/NIGHT

*The current carries fire toward Michael and Nadia. Even the
ice blocks are inflamed. So they are forced to dive deep into
the water and swim underneath the fire. They struggle in the
current, the fire above them blazing the dark water.*

*They find a spot on the surface and emerge. Breathless and
cold, they crawl to shore. Through the trees they see the burning west wall of the fortress. They stumble toward it, dazed,
shivering, Michael following the light obsessively.*

## 152. THE TARTAR CAMP - EXT/NIGHT

*Many Warriors launch boats into the river. The fires have
melted much of the ice blocking their way. From the battlements, Russians fire bullets into the Raiders, but the Tartars
are protected by night.*

## 153. THE FORTRESS - EXT/NIGHT

*Tartars reach the wall. Long ladders are lifted and they climb
up the walls. The Russians not fighting fires are able to push
the ladders off, and Warriors fall to their deaths. Other Warriors are burnt by the raining acyde in the cauldrons—and
by precise crossbow fire from the Russian Archers.*

*The Hordes keep trying to cross. General Yuragon commands the cannon to open fire, and many boats are blown out of the water.*

## 154. TARTAR CAMP - EXT/NIGHT

*The Khan is excited by the noise, the chaos, the blood-curdling screams of passion and torment and attack. Murga-Ti orders more flaming arrows shot. They hit the far wall across the river but bounce off. The flames filling the world glaze in Feofar Khan's eyes. He mounts his horse, waving his saber in ecstasy. He leads a charge of Horsemen onto the ice.*

*Murga-Ti watches with shock as the Khan slides from the burning ice into the water. He runs to the bank as the Khan is walking out, his sword held high in command as if nothing has happened. Boats burn in the river. More Archers fire silent dark arrows. Another horse is brought for the Khan, and he laughs as he mounts. Murga-Ti stares at him strangely.*

FEOFAR KHAN: Do not worry, Murga-Ti. We cannot be
　　　　　defeated. It is written that we shall rule the water,
　　　　　the air, the earth—the fire!

MURGA-TI: Roola is dead, my Lord. Our strategy is not
　　　　　working!

*But the Khan does not hear anything except his own mind. He rides through the camp to rally his tired, Wounded Warriors. Those that will not stand and fight he slashes with his saber.*

FEOFAR KHAN: Who will ride atop the water with me?
Who will ride through fire?

*Suddenly, bullets come through the darkness, and Tartars fall, blood spurting from their flesh. The Khan stares in confusion, then he turns toward the field—and hundreds of torches seem to be moving toward him—ghost-like Avengers of light! It's a strange sight.*

*General Nerensky and Major Torlov lead an Army of Russian Soldiers, Cossacks, and Refugees across the fields. Every Man has a torch and a gun, and they fire with accuracy! Mikhail and Jolivet are also with the Column.*

*Sprays of bullets scatter the Tartars. The surprise from the rear flank is complete. The Khan doesn't retreat. He sits astride his horse and stares. The Russians come closer—closer—and suddenly a volley of many bullets hit him at once. Blood spews from his face, neck, chest, arms. He keeps holding the reins of his horse, which twists in fear. More bullets strike Feofar Khan—it seems like hundreds—but he stays mounted and upright on his animal. The horse jerks his body, it races through the camp. The Khan slumps down over its neck, then is jerked up again in a hideous parody of motion. Somehow the reins and harness have tangled around the Khan's arms and thighs, the stirrups hold his legs. As the horse dashes away, the dead Feofar Khan goes with the spooked animal—a bleeding Body seeming to be alive as it rides off across the steppes.*

## 155. THE FORTRESS - EXT/NIGHT

*The Russian Soldiers on the wall yell with joy at the sight of the Czar's Reinforcements across the river. Major Alekim has tears of happiness in his eyes. General Yuragon smiles with satisfaction. He holds his pistol to the air and fires a volley in celebration.*

GENERAL YURAGON: Major! Go inform the Grand Duke that the city is saved.

MAJOR ALEKIM: Yes, sir! At once!

*The Young Soldier runs toward the central castle.*

*From the shadows, Zurevno witnesses the failure of his plans: The fires on the wall are being put out. The river fires are drowning in the current. The Tartars are being defeated in their own camp. And his Troops at the Bolchia Gate lie dead and rotting. Now Colonel Zurevno's face twists with hate and rage, and a maniacal foreboding. He glances up to the fortress and sees Grand Duke Theodore watching the world through his safe window.*

ZUREVNO: I will take you with me to Hell!

*He quickly moves in darkness toward the central fortress entrance.*

## 156. INNER CORRIDORS - INT/NIGHT

*Zurevno walks steadily, like a dignified Soldier. People pass him, nod, smile in acknowledgement. He hurries up stone steps, climbs to another floor. Now the passageway is empty.*

*He stops, unsure of the way. Major Alekim is coming his way, a broad smile on his face.*

MAJOR ALEKIM: We've beaten them, Strogoff!

ZUREVNO: Yes, sir.

*When the Major passes with his back turned, Zurevno pulls out his saber and slashes. The Young Major falls into a pool of his own blood. Zurevno keeps walking down the passageway toward the Grand Duke's quarters.*

## 157. NEAR THE BOLCHIA GATE - EXT/NIGHT

*Fire still rages near the west wall, but it's being contained. Michael and Nadia walk through the gate. They see the Bodies of Peter and the Bohemian dressed as Russians. They see Sangarre, her face melted by acyde. Old Louis is crushed under a horse.*

STROGOFF: Zurevno's plan succeeded!

NADIA: But Michael, they're dead!

STROGOFF: No. Something's wrong. Where is his body?

NADIA: It could be anywhere.

*Michael stares up at the fortress, his eye focusing hazily on the tall tower.*

*Wassili Fedor is smothering some dying flames. He wipes his brow—then suddenly sees his daughter. He stares, unsure, then yells.*

FEDOR: Nadia!

*She turns, shocked to see him. Her eyes fill with tears of joy. They embrace passionately.*

NADIA: Oh, Father!

FEDOR: You're safe! My child!

*Nadia smiles at him, then turns to introduce Michael.*

NADIA: Father, this is the man who helped me. Michael
      Strogoff—

*But Michael is no longer there. He has disappeared. Fedor looks at her tenderly.*

FEDOR: Yes. I have met Strogoff. The courier.

*She looks at him strangely.*

NADIA: You met him, Father? When?

FEDOR: When he arrived early this evening. But I asked about you, and he denied that he knew you.

*Suddenly the situation dawns on Nadia.*

NADIA: Oh, no! Father!

*She stares at the fortress, then tugs at him to follow her quickly.*

NADIA: He can't see!

## 158. INNER CORRIDORS - INT/NIGHT

*Zurevno hurries along, now very frustrated. He looks in rooms, other chambers. He finds the Maid, Maria, refilling a wash basin. She stares at him.*

MAID: A fine evening for victory, sir.

ZUREVNO: Where is the Grand Duke? Which chambers are his, Maria? I've lost my way, you see.

*She is silent, unsure what to say. Zurevno has no more patience. He grabs her violently by the throat.*

ZUREVNO: Where?

*The frightened Girl points down the passageway.*
*Zurevno smiles. He pulls Maria to him in an embrace, as if to kiss her—but she suddenly gasps and slumps in his arms.*

*He lowers her to the floor and jerks the saber from her stomach.*

*He runs down the last bit of corridor and leaps up the stairs.*

## 159. THE GRAND DUKE'S CHAMBERS - INT/NIGHT

*Zurevno slings open the door, his sword ready—but the room is empty! The only living thing is the golden nightingale. In a rage, Zurevno slashes the cage with the sword. It falls to the floor and the frightened bird flies out.*

*There is the large painting of the Czar and Czarina. Zurevno slashes this, also, and it falls off the wall. He continues to rip the canvas with the blade—*

ZUREVNO: Damn you! Damn you all!

*Then he hears a Familiar Voice behind him.*

STROGOFF: And damn you as well, Zurevno!

*Michael stands at the door, holding the two huge Siberian hunting knives, one in each hand. He stares at Zurevno—his vision: finally clear!*

*Zurevno screams in rage and charges, his saber slashing the air. Michael steps into him, blocks the saber with his knives. The Two Men are drawn together in a tight, close hold. They strain face-to-face. Zurevno suddenly smashes his forehead against Michael's eye-wound, causing him to back off in pain.*

*Zurevno attacks again. Michael recovers with another*

*block, but now his face bleeds. Zurevno slashes over Michael's head—he ducks—the nightingale screeches in the rafters—and Michael kicks out, his boot catching Zurevno in the shins. The Colonel falls against the Grand Duke's desk, knocking off the bottle of Fedor's acyde. The mixture burns into the floor.*

*Zurevno rises and takes a breath. The Two Men feint, stalk each other. Zurevno slashes his sword, and gashes Michael. Blood flows from his arm, but Michael blocks Zurevno's other thrust and smashes a knife-hilt into the Colonel's face. Zurevno reels away, his cheek dripping blood—*

## 160. THE GRAND DUKE'S PRIVATE CHAPEL - INT/NIGHT - AT THIS SAME TIME

*Theodore is on his knees praying before the Crucifix. Fedor and Nadia burst through the door. Behind them are Several Soldiers.*

GRAND DUKE: What is this?

FEDOR: Sire, my daughter has told me an incredible story! We must believe her!

NADIA: Where is the man who told you he was the courier?

GRAND DUKE: Strogoff?

NADIA: He is not! He's the impostor, Victor Zurevno!

GRAND DUKE: Child, are you mad?

*But they suddenly hear loud crashing noises from the floor above. The unmistakable sounds of fighting—*

## 161. GRAND DUKE'S CHAMBERS - INT/NIGHT

*The nightingale flies around the room in fear. Zurevno's saber cuts a huge arc. Michael watches carefully, looking for when Zurevno might drop his guard. He lunges at the Colonel, but Zurevno steps to the side and slices Michael again. The cuts are so deep that blood streams down his arm. He can hardly lift it.*

*Zurevno gloats, smiling his twisted grin. Now that Michael is vulnerable, Zurevno gains energy. He thrusts high, but then slashes down, cutting Michael's leg. Michael falls to a knee just inches from the burning pool of acyde. Zurevno picks up a huge chair and runs at him, smashing it on top of Michael. Then Zurevno hacks away with his sword, jabbing between the spaces of the wood—slashing away to try to hit flesh.*

*Michael lunges out and slices Zurevno's knee. The cut is deep. Zurevno screams and falls, then tries to stand. Michael throws the same chair back on him and Zurevno topples again. He drags his leg to get away. Michael leaps. Zurevno screams as he's shoved into the pool of acyde.*

*It burns his back. He kicks and scrambles, standing with a look of horror in his eyes. He grits his teeth in mad determination and charges Michael again. Michael dodges him, then rips a shield from the wall. He quickly whips his knife from behind it and throws—the blade sticking in Zurevno's side.*

*The Colonel staggers back, ripping the knife out. He has never let go of his sword, so he keeps swinging. Michael blocks with the shield. Both men are so bloody, so weak and torn apart—*

*But Zurevno seems to love the fight. It fuels him, brings him strange ecstatic pleasure—*

*Michael charges with the shield, and with the full force of his body plows into Zurevno. They both fall. The saber drops. Michael's fist pounds the Colonel's face. Every time either man grips the other's wound, a groan of pain surfaces. Michael weakens, having only one good arm—*

*Zurevno grips his throat. He begins to strangle Michael, who struggles desperately beneath him. Michael is losing breath. His wounded arm reaches out on the floor—his fingers search—and they feel the tip of Zurevno's saber. Inch-by-inch it comes to him—*

*With his other hand he holds Zurevno's arm, trying to rip the Colonel's hands from his throat. The clarity of his vision grows hazy—*

*The saber blade is sharp. Michael grips it in his fist and it slices through his hand. The tighter he holds it, the more it cuts him—but he's able to bring it close and wedge the blade between his chest and Zurevno—*

*The Colonel bangs Michael's head on the floor. He squeezes Michael's neck with all his power—Michael pushes his body upward from the floor, all his weight going into the pressure of the blade—one thorough thrust—*

*And Zurevno suddenly stops. His hands stay on Michael's neck, but his eyes glaze over. He stares down at Michael, a gurgling sound comes from his throat!*

*The Grand Duke, Nadia, Fedor, and the Soldiers burst*

*through the door. They're stunned by the sight of the Two Men on the floor in a pool of blood. The Grand Duke, confused, does not know whom to arrest. He screams out in a booming voice of command.*

GRAND DUKE: Colonel Zurevno!

*Zurevno slowly turns his face toward Theodore in acknowledgement, his lips forming into that evil grin—when blood pours out of his mouth. Victor Zurevno breathes his last!*

*Nadia runs to Michael and holds him carefully in her arms. The blood of his many wounds covers her, but she doesn't care.*

∽

## 162. THE FORTRESS - EXT/DAY

*The sun shines on a glorious morning. From the battlements, the terrain of battle is surveyed by Grand Duke Theodore, General Nerensky, General Yuragon, and Wassili Fedor.*

*The Journalist, Jolivet, sits on the wall with his paper, sketching a dark portrait of the aftermath of battle: the carnage upon the earth…bodies, dead horses, vultures.*

*He looks up from his work and sees Michael and Nadia walking quietly along the riverbank below.*

JOLIVET'S NARRATION [*voice-over*]: "I want to believe that some day the end of all wars will come. That some day all peoples will live together in harmony and respect. The madness I have witnessed, the cruelty, makes my dream darken. But then I observe the great love of Nadia Fedor and Michael Strogoff, and my dream of peace suddenly discovers light again."

*He watches Nadia and Michael take a small boat out into the river.*

## 163. ON THE RIVER - EXT/DAY

*The bright sun has melted some of the ice. They can row easily to the other side. Nadia does much of it since Michael's hand and arm are bandaged. He wears an eye-patch.*

## 164. TARTAR CAMPSITE - EXT/DAY

*They land the boat where the Russian Soldiers continue to round up Prisoners. Many Tartars are shot by Firing Squads. Major Torlov is in command. Mounds of dead Bodies are being piled and burned. The smoke rises to the sky. Nadia and Michael watch grimly.*

*Mikhail and other Refugee Troops herd the Tartar Women and Children. They are set free. A Long Caravan of them wanders away toward the steppes. On a weak horse, one particular "Old Woman" in robes and veils looks back. It is Murga-Ti in disguise, his horse being led by the Asian Dancer.*

## 165. FAR DOWN THE RIVERBANK - EXT/DAY

*Nadia and Michael sit in the grass. He is so hurt that Nadia must help prop him up against a tree. She kisses his bandaged hand. They quietly watch the warm sun filter down through the trees…they watch it glisten on the rippling river. Nadia lays her head on Michael's shoulder, he caresses her long hair.*

*For a while they are at peace and can rest.*

∾

# MICHAEL STROGOFF
## A Screenplay

### THOMAS ROBERDEAU
With an Introduction by Paul Schmidt

*Michael Strogoff* is an exotic adventure tale set in mid-nineteenth century Russia during the violent conflicts between the Czar's Cossack army and the raging Tartar hordes. Based on the famed Jules Verne novel, this is a classic spy story and romance, focusing on the dramatic odyssey of the soldier, Michael—a brave courier—and his beautiful lover, Nadia.

Taking on a near-impossible mission, Michael Strogoff encounters a universe of treachery, turmoil, and bloodshed, as he travels across the wind-swept steppes, rivers, and snowy mountains of the Russian land. Michael's choices, and the series of events that result, create a harrowing drama of conscience, survival, intrigue, and faith set against his passionate love for Nadia. *Michael Strogoff* is a grand adventure that has been filmed in the past because of Verne's compelling epic scope. This new verison appeals to contemporary tastes because of its focus on the psychological natures of the characters, the fast-paced action, its visual panorama of magnificent landscapes, and its lavish spectacle.

Thomas Roberdeau has worked for many years in motion pictures, television, theater, and literature. His films, screenplays, and photographs have received recognition from the National Endowment for the Arts, the American Film Institute, the California Arts Council, the Council on International Nontheatrical Events, and the Corporation for Public Broadcasting.